701 MORE SENTENCE SERMONS

701 MORE SENTENCE SERMONS

Attention-Getting Quotes for
Church Signs, Bulletins,
Newsletters, and Sermons

L. James Harvey

Kregel
Publications

701 More Sentence Sermons: Attention-Getting Quotes for Church Signs, Bulletins, Newsletters, and Sermons

Published by Kregel Publications, a division of Kregel, Inc., P.O. Box 2607, Grand Rapids, MI 49501. Kregel Publications provides trusted, biblical publications for Christian growth and service. Your comments and suggestions are valued.

For more information about Kregel Publications, visit our web site: www.kregel.com.

Unless noted below, Scripture quotations are from the *Holy Bible, New International Version®*. © 1973, 1978, 1984 by International Bible Society. Used by permission of Zondervan Publishing House. All rights reserved.

Sentence sermons 635, 646, 661, 681, 687, and 697 are the author's own translation.

Sentence sermons 636 and 638 are from *The New King James Version*. © 1979, 1980, 1982, Thomas Nelson, Inc., Publishers.

Sentence sermon 682 is from the *New American Standard Bible,* © the Lockman Foundation 1960, 1962, 1963, 1968, 1971, 1972, 1973, 1975, 1977.

Cover design © 2002 by Kregel Publications

ISBN 0-8254-2888-2

Printed in the United States of America

02 03 04 05 / 5 4 3 2 1

This book is dedicated to the thousands of pastors and churches who have caught the vision. They see how effectively a church sign ministry can carry out the Great Commission.

Contents

Acknowledgments

Since publication of *701 Sentence Sermons*, people have sent me many more sentence sermons. In addition, people who know of our church sign ministry here in Maryland regularly pass along new material that they have found. Below are some of the people who have contributed "sermons" to this collection and who encourage me in the effort.

Ann Aurich
Merilee J. Bailey
Malinda Banks
Linda Brubaker
Russell Briley
Joy Butler
Bob and Bette Cantile
Mark Engelmann
Lisa Harvey
Debby Herr
Chuck and Ruth Long
Rodger Loveing

Phillip Massey
Steve Nicholas
Judy and Shawn McCloskey
Marty Martin
Mary Ellen Merlino
Willie Miller
Charlcie Olivier
Linda Sadeghi
Donn Stansbury
Elsie Taylor
Jim and Sharon Zoeteway

. . . and last but not least, my wife, Jackie Harvey, the editor, chief speller, and cheerleader for the project.

Part One

CHAPTER 1

The History of Signs

The earliest signs along the path surely were carved into trees or chiseled out of rock to provide directions to travelers. In the road systems of ancient Babylon, and later of Rome, signs along the road noted distances to various destinations. How far we have come, with an estimated 55 million traffic signs in the United States alone!

Early signs conveyed information in picture and symbol. Only when literacy became relatively common could words be used effectively. Those earlier symbols were chosen because their meanings were quickly and universally recognized. A bunch of grapes announced shops where wine was available. Three gold balls was the symbol for a pawnbroker.

In the ruins of Ephesus, my wife and I noticed a sign carved in stone on the main street that pointed travelers to the library at the center of the city.

On the whitewashed wall of one ancient Roman building, an advertisement for a lodging and eating establishment can be seen. At executions, the Romans placed placards on crosses informing passersby of the crime for which the condemned was being crucified. Christians will remember that when Jesus was crucified, a sign above his head announced that he was "King of the Jews." Caiaphas, the high priest, was turned down when he asked that Pilate change the sign to, "He said he was the king of the Jews." The biblical story helps us understand this use of signs in the first century.

So, permanent signs in the ancient world were carved in wood or stone to give people directions and to identify buildings, cities, and points of importance. Later, signs were painted on walls. The invention of movable type and the printing press by Johannes Gutenberg led to a quantum step forward for written communication. Most signs still were etched into wood and stone, but the more temporary variety could now be printed.

Early church signs also were carved in stone. Those that survive tend to record the name of the church and the year it was founded. But within the last century, the development of individual movable letters permitted churches the luxury of changing their messages to the outside world. The new technology in information boards allowed a congregation to announce, in addition to the name and date of the church, the name of the pastor and times of services. They could advertise the Sunday sermon title each week and publicize special events.

A lot of information was included on these changeable announcement boards, which were attached to the building or planted beside it, almost always with its face parallel to the street. People read the board as they walked by or passed in a carriage or early automobile. This kind of installation did not work so well when automobiles and the pace of life quickened. The speed at which people passed church buildings increased significantly.

Effective signs today must face the direction from which traffic is coming to allow more reading time. Signs work best when moved as close to the street as is practical without obstructing visibility. Even then, in a car traveling at thirty-five miles an hour, the driver has, at most, four or five seconds to digest a sign's message.

Church signs seem to be a particularly North American phenomenon, although the more traditional installations are common in the United Kingdom and Australia. They are not seen much in other parts of the world. Maybe this is because America is wedded to the automobile for transportation and has a well-maintained network of roads. It may also be due, in part, to differences in the cultures of other nations, which may not be as oriented toward public communication. Signs are rarely found in front of mosques, and those synagogue signs that do exist tend to give minimal information.

In any case, a lot more can be done with signs in the United States and Canada.

Americans may be attracted to signs that provide important, abbreviated information, information that can be gathered and processed on the run. For whatever reason, signs are omnipresent. My wife and I frequently walk along a route that winds through neighborhoods of single-family homes, townhouses, and apartments. One day, when I was walking the route alone, I decided to count the number of signs I saw. Within about one and one-half miles I had counted 250, not including house numbers or parking-space designations. Later, I asked my wife to guess how many signs stood near the streets that she had walked many times. She guessed that there might be about ten. Her response reminded me that signs have become so common that we generally take in their meanings without even acknowledging their presence.

One student of church signs theorizes that the watershed event for their development came in the late 1960s when a company produced an easily changed, backlit message board with letters large enough to be easily read by motorists. Whatever the impetus, church signs have proliferated.

Churches with an active sign program report that visitors frequently come to worship simply because they were intrigued by something they read on the church sign. One estimate is that the expense of a sophisticated sign can be recovered in the giving of the new attendees it brings in within five years. The experience of our church over a five-year period fits that hypothesis.

The primary reason for installing an effective church sign should be that it allows for the presentation of God's truth in a new way. Urban churches and those along major highways may have a daily traffic flow in the thousands. Many of these are people who, as Thoreau said, are "living lives of quiet desperation." A bit of God's truth at the right time can make all the difference in their lives. As Christians, we believe that the Holy Spirit is at work, and we believe that God will use His truth when we display it for people to see and consider.

Traditional sermons are important in the life of any church, but they reach only those who attend a service. A sentence sermon on a church sign can reach thousands of unbelievers every day. Why would any church pass up such a ministry opportunity? Stories of how sign messages have changed people's lives and saved at least one man's life, are reported in my book *701 Sentence Sermons*.

A large church near our home has built facilities along a major divided highway with a heavy traffic flow. A school is attached to the church building. There are two major entrances to the property off the highway, one with a stoplight. The church has at least a quarter mile of frontage and a fantastic opportunity to place a sign near the stoplight. Instead of taking the opportunity to spread God's truth through an effective sign ministry, the church has a painted sign listing times of services. The letters are too small to be read unless one stops or enters their driveway. What an opportunity missed. It can't be a lack of money. The congregation's giving averages twenty thousand dollars a week. A top-quality sign could be raised there for seven thousand dollars or less and would likely pay for itself within a short time. This church supports a number of missionaries in different parts of the world but seems unaware of the unchurched thousands who pass by their building each day.

How many other churches are missing a golden opportunity to present God's truth to passersby who desperately need to have it? Too many, I'm afraid. Fortunately, the number of churches developing effective sign ministries is growing rapidly.

CHAPTER 2

How to Kill a Church Sign Ministry

If we assume that a church sign ministry is a good thing and that it presents a viable way to spread God's truth, we can also expect that Satan will find ways to compromise its effectiveness. Below are some of the ways a church's sign ministry can be killed. Any church wishing to have an effective sign ministry should avoid these deadly diseases.

Using Letters That Are Too Small

Nothing kills a sign's effectiveness more than having letters too small to be read by passing motorists. This is the single most serious mistake churches make. Test your sign and sign letter size before the board is ordered and installed. Make a chart of different sized letters and drive by at various speeds to test the ease with which each can be read. A sign company executive remarked that he had never heard of a church complaining that the letters they had ordered were too large, but quite a few complain of letters that are too small. Remember that many people passing by are elderly, have restricted eyesight, or do not read well for some other reason. If you have already made this mistake, it may be worth the expense of changing your sign and letter size. It's better to correct the problem and have an effective sign than to frustrate passersby who want to read your sign and can't.

Misspelled Words

Misspelled words are a distraction. They rob attention from the message, and they reflect poorly on the church. Unless you are an excellent speller, it is wise to keep a small dictionary with the sign letters and, when in doubt, to check the spelling of your message.

Failure to Set Agreed-Upon Policies

Without a well-worked-out plan from the start, problems creep in. A policy statement should be written out dictating when the sign is to be changed, who is to select the message, and who is to put it up. This policy statement is the way content problems, like those below, can be resolved as soon as they arise.

Vanity Messages

The work of the sign is to present God's truth, not to puff up egos. Congratulations and announcements of anniversaries, birthdays, and graduations can quickly get out of hand, leaving very little space for the truths you want to spread.

Obstructed View

Two nearby congregations have effective sign ministries, but trees and vines have grown and now diminish sight lines. Motorists have less time to read the messages. Strategic landscape trimming usually solves the problem. One winter, a storm left our church sign obstructed by a huge mound of plowed snow. A church member used an axe to cut away at the pile until visibility was restored. Another visual problem is inadequate illumination. Check frequently to ensure that lights are functioning and are properly positioned so that the sign can be read day and night.

Controversial Messages

Churches should unapologetically present God's truth, but some messages invite problems. In Washington, D.C., a United Methodist church posted the message, "WAS IT ADAM AND EVE OR ADAM AND STEVE? GENESIS 2:18–25." A number of homosexuals lived nearby. Within hours, the city trucked away the sign, claiming that the church had not obtained the necessary permits to erect it. The church had a building permit, and the city had mentioned no other required approvals. However, when the gay community complained, the city suddenly discovered that a permit from the historic district was necessary. The city's speed in acting against the church was un-precedented. A year later, the church still didn't have its sign back, and it was embroiled in an ongoing legal action. Another church placed a message implying that work was a good cure for welfare. People complained that this was offensive to welfare recipients, and the sign soon was vandalized. Churches need to present God's truth boldly, but tact and diplomacy can preserve a sign ministry.

Failure to Change Messages

Signs need to be changed often enough that the driving public will keep an eye on the board, awaiting its next message. The most common practice is to set one day each week (often each Sunday or Monday) to change the message. Some people go out of their way to pass meaningful signs. It is helpful if they have confidence that a new message will be up on a given day.

Failure to Use Opportunities

Current events and seasons of the year offer special opportunities for sign ministries. Signs will seem to lack relevance if they fail to capitalize on these occasions. After the terrible World Trade Center tragedy on September 11, 2001, people were looking for words of comfort. They were paying attention to spiritual messages that they normally would have ignored. Our church and others around us changed our sign messages immediately to speak to our community. The school shootings of recent years offered similar chances to be heard with fresh understanding. Shocked people look for healing. Regular holidays, especially Christmas and Easter, present times for focused messages. It's important to use these opportunities for an effective sign ministry.

Running out of Needed Letters

Nothing is more frustrating than having a great message to post but lacking one letter to complete it. Stock enough letters to meet needs. Sign companies will recommend the number of each letter you should have. Our experience is that it's best to go beyond their recommendations and to order two or three extras of each vowel as well as a few extra *T*s, *R*s, and *S*s.

Sign ministries have proven effective, and there are numerous testimonies as to how people's lives have been saved and changed. However, we can expect that any positive ministry will be attacked by the adversary, and an attempt will be made to neutralize it. With some intelligent effort, we can make sentence sermons as effective as possible and avoid the problems that can kill and weaken them.

CHAPTER 3

How to Use This Book

Because people's interests, needs, and interpretations may differ, a variety of sentence sermons have been presented in the pages that follow. Some are humorous, some are straightforward, and still others are designed to make people think. Some come from Scripture, some from Christian thinkers, and others from secular sources that present basic truths. People will react differently to the same sentence sermon depending on their perceptions and theological perspectives. Careful selection is essential to avoid controversy.

Churches will differ in their choice of sentence sermons depending on their location, the character of the majority of people who pass the church (e.g., their educational level, socioeconomic background, religious affiliation or lack of it), and the primary purpose of their sign.

If you are part of a church committee charged with the responsibility of a church sign, you can use the following rating system to select sermons that will be the best for your individual circumstances. Committee members can each take a book and rate every sentence sermon on the five-point rating scale presented here, circling the number that best indicates how they feel about it. For example, if they think the sermon is outstanding and should have priority, they can circle the 5. If it is very good, but there are better ones that should be used first, they can circle the 4. Those of less merit can be rated 3 and 2, with the understanding that they will be used after all the 4s and 5s. The 1 should be reserved for those not wanted at all. It is the veto rating.

The recommended scale is as follows:

1	2	3	4	5
(Poor)	(Weak)	(Average)	(Very Good)	(Best)
Do not use	Use others first	Use 4s & 5s first	Use 5s first	Use first

After each committee member has rated all of the sentence sermons, one of the members can average out the results, producing a list your committee feels is best for your situation. The high-priority messages can then be given to your sign master.

If you are an individual using the sentence sermons in one of the many other ways mentioned earlier, you can use the same rating system for yourself. This will help you readily identify those messages you most want to use and allow you to locate them easily and quickly.

Read, enjoy, and use the sentence sermons that follow!

Part Two

Part Two

CHAPTER 4

701 More Sentence Sermons

1.   **HERE'S YOUR LINK
                          TO ETERNITY—
                          WWW.JESUS.GOD**

Rating: 1   2   3   4   5   Date Used:

2.   **GOING TO WASTE?
                          ASK GOD TO
                          RECYCLE YOU**

Rating: 1   2   3   4   5   Date Used:

3.   **YOU CAN'T GET AHEAD
                          IF YOU'RE ALWAYS
                          TRYING TO GET EVEN**

Rating: 1   2   3   4   5   Date Used:

4.   **WRINKLED BY LIFE?
                          COME TO GOD
                          FOR A FAITH LIFT**

Rating: 1   2   3   4   5   Date Used:

5.
           IF PSYCHICS KNOW
           SO MUCH
           WHY DON'T THEY
           WIN THE LOTTERY?

Rating: 1   2   3   4   5   Date Used:

6.
           TO SAVE FACE
           KEEP THE
           LOWER PART SHUT

Rating: 1   2   3   4   5   Date Used:

7.
           PRAYER IS THE PAUSE
           THAT EMPOWERS

Rating: 1   2   3   4   5   Date Used:

8.
           IN UNFAILING LOVE
           GOD LEADS PEOPLE
           HE HAS REDEEMED

Rating: 1   2   3   4   5   Date Used:

9.
           IT'S NOT THE HEAT
           IT'S THE HUMILITY
           THAT COUNTS

Rating: 1   2   3   4   5   Date Used:

10.
           CHILDREN OF GOD—
           PLEASE CALL HOME
           YOUR FATHER
           IS WAITING

Rating: 1   2   3   4   5   Date Used:

11. **ONLY AN ACCORDION
SHOULD PLAY BOTH
ENDS AGAINST
THE MIDDLE**

Rating: 1   2   3   4   5   Date Used:

12. **LAUGHTER IS GOD'S
HAND ON THE
SHOULDER OF A
TROUBLED WORLD**

Rating: 1   2   3   4   5   Date Used:

13. **PRAISE GOD
IN YOUR TRIALS
TURN BURDENS
INTO BLESSINGS**

Rating: 1   2   3   4   5   Date Used:

14. **WHEN ALL ELSE FAILS
DO THE RIGHT THING**

Rating: 1   2   3   4   5   Date Used:

15. **DO THE RIGHT THING
NOT THE
COMFORTABLE THING**

Rating: 1   2   3   4   5   Date Used:

16. **PRIDE KILLS
FAITH IN GOD**

Rating: 1   2   3   4   5   Date Used:

17.

A PINT OF EXAMPLE
IS WORTH A GALLON
OF ADVICE

Rating: 1   2   3   4   5   Date Used:

18.

LOVE CURES PEOPLE—
THOSE WHO RECEIVE
AND THOSE WHO GIVE

Rating: 1   2   3   4   5   Date Used:

19.

FOR ALL YOU DO
HIS BLOOD'S FOR YOU

Rating: 1   2   3   4   5   Date Used:

20.

THE MOST HIGHLY
INFLAMMABLE WOOD
IS A CHIP
ON THE SHOULDER

Rating: 1   2   3   4   5   Date Used:

21.

WAR DOESN'T
DETERMINE WHO
IS RIGHT—
JUST WHO IS LEFT

Rating: 1   2   3   4   5   Date Used:

22.

IT'S EASY TO TELL
SINNER FROM SAINT
—SINNER IS ALWAYS
THE ONE YOU AIN'T

Rating: 1   2   3   4   5   Date Used:

23.
YOU'RE ONLY YOUNG ONCE—AFTER THAT YOU NEED SOME OTHER EXCUSE

Rating: 1   2   3   4   5   Date Used:

24.
THERE'S NO FOOL LIKE AN OLD FOOL YOU CAN'T BEAT EXPERIENCE

Rating: 1   2   3   4   5   Date Used:

25.
PROFITING FROM ADVICE TAKES MORE WISDOM THAN GIVING IT

Rating: 1   2   3   4   5   Date Used:

26.
THE HAPPIEST PEOPLE ARE TOO BUSY TO KNOW IT

Rating: 1   2   3   4   5   Date Used:

27.
HUMILITY: IF YOU KNOW YOU HAVE IT YOU'VE LOST IT

Rating: 1   2   3   4   5   Date Used:

28.
MONEY TALKS— IT USUALLY SAYS GOODBYE

Rating: 1   2   3   4   5   Date Used:

29.

THE HEAVIEST
THING TO CARRY
IS A GRUDGE

Rating: 1   2   3   4   5   Date Used:

30.

HOW DO YOU WANT
TO SPEND ETERNITY?
SMOKING OR
NON-SMOKING?

Rating: 1   2   3   4   5   Date Used:

31.

IDEAS DON'T WORK
UNLESS YOU DO

Rating: 1   2   3   4   5   Date Used:

32.

CHRISTIANITY IS NOT
BELIEVING THE
IMPOSSIBLE BUT
DOING THE INCREDIBLE

Rating: 1   2   3   4   5   Date Used:

33.

MAKE NEW FRIENDS
AND KEEP THE OLD—
ONE IS SILVER
THE OTHER GOLD

Rating: 1   2   3   4   5   Date Used:

34.

SUCCESS IS FINDING A
JOB THAT REALLY IS
WORTH DOING WELL

Rating: 1   2   3   4   5   Date Used:

35.
THE SON SHINES ON
THE RIGHTEOUS

Rating: 1 2 3 4 5 Date Used:

36.
ONE DOES NOT BELIEVE
WHO DOES NOT LIVE
THE BELIEF

Rating: 1 2 3 4 5 Date Used:

37.
ETERNAL FIRE INSURANCE
AVAILABLE HERE
FREE!

Rating: 1 2 3 4 5 Date Used:

38.
SAFETY RULES ARE
NOT SUPPOSED TO BE
LEARNED BY ACCIDENT

Rating: 1 2 3 4 5 Date Used:

39.
SOME PEOPLE ARE LIKE
TEA BAGS—THEY WORK
BEST IN HOT WATER

Rating: 1 2 3 4 5 Date Used:

40.
GOD RULES BY LOVE
NOT BY FORCE

Rating: 1 2 3 4 5 Date Used:

41.
REVENGE QUENCHES
EMOTIONS NO MORE
THAN SALT WATER
QUENCHES THIRST

Rating: 1 2 3 4 5 Date Used:

42.
A WISE PERSON HEARS THE WORDS OF GOD AND PUTS THEM INTO PRACTICE

Rating: 1   2   3   4   5   Date Used:

43.
MEDITATE ON THE WORD OF GOD— HIS TRUTH WORKS

Rating: 1   2   3   4   5   Date Used:

44.
MOST PEOPLE WANT TO SERVE GOD— IN AN ADVISORY CAPACITY

Rating: 1   2   3   4   5   Date Used:

45.
THE WINDS CANNOT BLOW DOWN A TREE THAT IS ROOTED IN GOD

Rating: 1   2   3   4   5   Date Used:

46.
ULTIMATE SUCCESS DEPENDS ON LOVING THINGS ABOVE MORE THAN THINGS BELOW

Rating: 1   2   3   4   5   Date Used:

47.
SIN'S WAGES = DEATH GOD'S WAGES = PEACE AND EVERLASTING LIFE

Rating: 1   2   3   4   5   Date Used:

48.
**YOUR CONSCIENCE
IS GOD SPEAKING
IGNORE AT
YOUR PERIL**

Rating: 1   2   3   4   5   Date Used:

49.
**I MAY READ MANY
BOOKS BUT THE
BIBLE READS ME**

Rating: 1   2   3   4   5   Date Used:

50.
**A BIG PERSON
GOES ON DESPITE
BIG DISCOURAGEMENT**

Rating: 1   2   3   4   5   Date Used:

51.
**OPEN MINDS
LIKE OPEN MOUTHS
SHOULD ONLY CLOSE
ON SOMETHING SOLID**

Rating: 1   2   3   4   5   Date Used:

52.
**THERE MUST BE AN
EMPTYING BEFORE
THERE CAN BE
A FILLING**

Rating: 1   2   3   4   5   Date Used:

53.
**THE SPIRIT-FILLED
LIFE IS LIFE AT ITS
VERY BEST**

Rating: 1   2   3   4   5   Date Used:

54.

JESUS DIDN'T GO AROUND KNOCKING PEOPLE DOWN —HE LIFTED THEM UP

Rating: 1   2   3   4   5   Date Used:

55.

TEMPER GETS US INTO TROUBLE BUT PRIDE KEEPS US THERE

Rating: 1   2   3   4   5   Date Used:

56.

THE HOLY SPIRIT EQUIPS US TO KEEP SIN OUT OF OUR LIFE

Rating: 1   2   3   4   5   Date Used:

57.

GOD IS THE AUTHOR OF SUCCESS

Rating: 1   2   3   4   5   Date Used:

58.

GOALS BASED ON GOD'S PROMISES LEAD TO SUCCESS

Rating: 1   2   3   4   5   Date Used:

59.

THE GREATEST DECEPTION IS TO EQUATE SUCCESS WITH WEALTH

Rating: 1   2   3   4   5   Date Used:

60.

ATTITUDES SHAPE FUTURES

Rating: 1   2   3   4   5   Date Used:

61.

GOD'S BLESSINGS
ARE BY-PRODUCTS
NOT TARGETS

Rating: 1   2   3   4   5   Date Used:

62.

GOD USES US—
WE DON'T USE HIM

Rating: 1   2   3   4   5   Date Used:

63.

NO ONE CARES HOW
MUCH YOU KNOW
UNTIL THEY KNOW
HOW MUCH YOU CARE

Rating: 1   2   3   4   5   Date Used:

64.

ASK NOT WHAT GOD
CAN DO FOR YOU
—ASK WHAT YOU
CAN DO FOR GOD

Rating: 1   2   3   4   5   Date Used:

65.

HONESTY PAYS
FAR MORE
THAN IT COSTS

Rating: 1   2   3   4   5   Date Used:

66.

AGE IS AN ISSUE OF
MIND OVER MATTER
IF YOU DON'T MIND
IT DOESN'T MATTER

Rating: 1   2   3   4   5   Date Used:

67.

**SMILE
GOD LOVES YOU!**

Rating: 1   2   3   4   5   Date Used:

68.

**WHEN YOU KNOW
HOW TO DIE
YOU KNOW
HOW TO LIVE**

Rating: 1   2   3   4   5   Date Used:

69.

**THE BEST THINGS
IN LIFE
AREN'T THINGS**

Rating: 1   2   3   4   5   Date Used:

70.

**GOD'S GRACE
IS THE ONLY CURE
FOR OUR SIN**

Rating: 1   2   3   4   5   Date Used:

71.

**FOLLOWING GOD'S
DIRECTIONS IS THE
ONLY WAY TO GET
SAFELY HOME**

Rating: 1   2   3   4   5   Date Used:

72.

**SIN ENOUGH AND
YOU WILL BECOME
DEAD TO IT**

Rating: 1   2   3   4   5   Date Used:

73.

**ENDURANCE IS NOT
BEARING THE HARD
THING BUT TURNING
IT INTO GLORY**

Rating: 1   2   3   4   5   Date Used:

74.

**CONSCIENCE SHOULD
NOT BE GUIDED
BY THE GALLUP POLL**

Rating: 1   2   3   4   5   Date Used:

75.

**USE ALL THE BRAINS
YOU HAVE PLUS ALL
YOU CAN BORROW**

Rating: 1   2   3   4   5   Date Used:

76.

**IT'S BETTER TO
SWALLOW ANGRY
WORDS THAN TO
HAVE TO EAT THEM**

Rating: 1   2   3   4   5   Date Used:

77.

**CHILDREN CAN READ
MAKE-BELIEVE FAITH
IN THEIR PARENTS**

Rating: 1   2   3   4   5   Date Used:

78.

**WHAT YOU BELIEVE
ABOUT GOD
IS THE SIGNIFICANT
THING ABOUT YOU**

Rating: 1   2   3   4   5   Date Used:

79.

THANKSGIVING IN ALL SITUATIONS IS GOD'S WILL FOR YOU IN CHRIST

Rating: 1 2 3 4 5 Date Used:

80.

HIGH INTEGRITY IS A BASIC CONDITION FOR HAPPINESS

Rating: 1 2 3 4 5 Date Used:

81.

SELF-LOVE SEEKS TO USE GOD— TRUE LOVE SEEKS TO PLEASE GOD

Rating: 1 2 3 4 5 Date Used:

82.

EGOISM IS THE MOST DANGEROUS OF PARASITES—IT KILLS TRUE LOVE

Rating: 1 2 3 4 5 Date Used:

83.

COURAGE IS FEAR THAT HAS SAID ITS PRAYERS

Rating: 1 2 3 4 5 Date Used:

84.

IT IS IN GOD— NOT THE DOW— THAT WE TRUST

Rating: 1 2 3 4 5 Date Used:

85.

**NOTHING THAT IS
DONE FOR GOD
IS EVER LOST**

Rating:　　　1　2　3　4　5　　　Date Used:

86.

**THE LAW DETECTS
GRACE CORRECTS**

Rating:　　　1　2　3　4　5　　　Date Used:

87.

**FOR BELIEVERS
ETERNAL LIFE HAS
ALREADY BEGUN**

Rating:　　　1　2　3　4　5　　　Date Used:

88.

**THOSE WHO JUDGE
HAVE NO TIME
TO LOVE**

Rating:　　　1　2　3　4　5　　　Date Used:

89.

**TRUE PEACE
IS FOUND ONLY
IN JESUS CHRIST**

Rating:　　　1　2　3　4　5　　　Date Used:

90.

**GOD'S TAPE MEASURE
GOES AROUND HEARTS
RATHER THAN HEADS**

Rating:　　　1　2　3　4　5　　　Date Used:

91.

**IF YOU'RE WAITING
FOR SOMETHING
TO TURN UP
TRY YOUR SLEEVES**

Rating:　　　1　2　3　4　5　　　Date Used:

92.

**PEOPLE FAIL IF THEIR
WISHBONE IS WHERE
THEIR BACKBONE
SHOULD BE**

Rating: 1   2   3   4   5   Date Used:

93.

**FRIENDS ARE LIKE
ELEVATOR BUTTONS
—THEY TAKE YOU UP
OR DOWN**

Rating: 1   2   3   4   5   Date Used:

94.

**YOUR CHARACTER
IS WHAT YOU DO
WHEN NO ONE
IS WATCHING**

Rating: 1   2   3   4   5   Date Used:

95.

**WISDOM IS HAVING
LOTS TO SAY
BUT NOT SAYING IT**

Rating: 1   2   3   4   5   Date Used:

96.

**MARRIAGE SHOULD
BE A DUET—
NOT A DUEL**

Rating: 1   2   3   4   5   Date Used:

97.

**THE MIGHTY OAK
WAS ONCE A NUT THAT
STOOD ITS GROUND**

Rating: 1   2   3   4   5   Date Used:

98.

**THE TONGUE WEIGHS
VERY LITTLE BUT FEW
PEOPLE CAN HOLD IT**

Rating: 1   2   3   4   5   Date Used:

99.

**SPEND MORE TIME
COUNTING BLESSINGS
THAN ADDING UP
YOUR TROUBLES**

Rating: 1   2   3   4   5   Date Used:

100.

**A FEW WORDS
OF LOVE CAN MAKE
A WORLD
OF DIFFERENCE**

Rating: 1   2   3   4   5   Date Used:

101.

**A MAN IS RICH BASED
ON WHAT HE IS—
NOT WHAT HE HAS**

Rating: 1   2   3   4   5   Date Used:

102.

**SUCCESS COMES
IN CANS —
FAILURE COMES
IN CAN'TS**

Rating: 1   2   3   4   5   Date Used:

103.

**BE THE LABOR
GREAT OR SMALL
DO IT WELL
OR NOT AT ALL**

Rating: 1   2   3   4   5   Date Used:

104. **TIME IS MORE VALUABLE THAN MONEY BECAUSE IT IS IRREPLACEABLE**

Rating: 1   2   3   4   5   Date Used:

105. **TO FORGET YOUR PROBLEMS BE THERE TO HELP OTHERS SOLVE THEIRS**

Rating: 1   2   3   4   5   Date Used:

106. **BE MORE CONCERNED ABOUT GOD'S OPINION THAN ABOUT WHAT OTHERS WILL THINK**

Rating: 1   2   3   4   5   Date Used:

107. **THE BEST WAY TO GET THE LAST WORD IS TO APOLOGIZE**

Rating: 1   2   3   4   5   Date Used:

108. **THE TRAIN OF FAILURE OFTEN RUNS ON THE TRACK OF LAZINESS**

Rating: 1   2   3   4   5   Date Used:

109. **TO FIND DIRECTION FROM GOD YOU MUST TAKE CORRECTION FROM GOD**

Rating: 1   2   3   4   5   Date Used:

110.

**BRING SUNSHINE
TO OTHERS AND YOU
WILL NEVER LIVE
IN THE SHADOWS**

Rating: 1 2 3 4 5   Date Used:

111.

**BUSYNESS
DOES NOT EQUAL
PRODUCTIVENESS**

Rating: 1 2 3 4 5   Date Used:

112.

**TO BE SUCCESSFUL
FOLLOW THE ADVICE
YOU GIVE TO OTHERS**

Rating: 1 2 3 4 5   Date Used:

113.

**TOO MANY PEOPLE QUIT
LOOKING FOR WORK
WHEN THEY FIND A JOB**

Rating: 1 2 3 4 5   Date Used:

114.

**ABILITY TAKES YOU
TO THE TOP
BUT CHARACTER
KEEPS YOU THERE**

Rating: 1 2 3 4 5   Date Used:

115.

**YOUR WORDS
ARE A WINDOW
TO YOUR HEART**

Rating: 1 2 3 4 5   Date Used:

116.

**A SHUT MOUTH
GATHERS NO FOOT**

Rating: 1   2   3   4   5   Date Used:

117.

**JESUS KNOWS ALL
OUR FAULTS AND
LOVES US STILL**

Rating: 1   2   3   4   5   Date Used:

118.

**PICK YOUR FRIENDS
BUT NOT TO PIECES**

Rating: 1   2   3   4   5   Date Used:

119.

**IF YOU CAN READ
THIS SIGN YOU CAN
STILL BE FORGIVEN**

Rating: 1   2   3   4   5   Date Used:

120.

**THE MOST VALUABLE
GIFT YOU CAN
GIVE ANOTHER IS
A GOOD EXAMPLE**

Rating: 1   2   3   4   5   Date Used:

121.

**A MINUTE OF THOUGHT
IS WORTH MORE THAN
AN HOUR OF TALK**

Rating: 1   2   3   4   5   Date Used:

122.

**IT'S NOT THE
HOURS YOU PUT IN
IT'S WHAT YOU PUT IN
THE HOURS**

Rating: 1   2   3   4   5   Date Used:

123.

**ONE GETS DOG TIRED
AT NIGHT FROM
GROWLING ALL DAY**

Rating: 1   2   3   4   5   Date Used:

124.

**JESUS IS A FRIEND
WHO STAYS WHEN THE
WORLD WALKS OUT**

Rating: 1   2   3   4   5   Date Used:

125.

**JUMPING
TO CONCLUSIONS
IS BAD EXERCISE**

Rating: 1   2   3   4   5   Date Used:

126.

**THE CLOCK
PASSES TIME
BY KEEPING
ITS HANDS BUSY**

Rating: 1   2   3   4   5   Date Used:

127.

**IN CIVILIZED LIFE
LAW FLOATS
IN A SEA OF ETHICS
—EARL WARREN**

Rating: 1   2   3   4   5   Date Used:

128.

**THE BEGINNING OF
TRUE FAITH IS THE
END OF ANXIETY
— GEORGE MULLER**

Rating: 1   2   3   4   5   Date Used:

129.   **OUR GREATEST NEED IS
NOT TO DO THINGS, BUT
TO BELIEVE THINGS
—OSWALD CHAMBERS**

Rating: 1   2   3   4   5   Date Used:

130.   **ADVERSITY DOTH BEST
DISCOVER VIRTUE
—FRANCIS BACON**

Rating: 1   2   3   4   5   Date Used:

131.   **GOD IS GENEROUS
—THE CROSS IS
THE SIGN OF ADDITION
—G. SWEETING**

Rating: 1   2   3   4   5   Date Used:

132.   **LOVE BUILT ON BEAUTY
SOON AS BEAUTY
DIES
—JOHN DONNE**

Rating: 1   2   3   4   5   Date Used:

133.   **YOU CAN TELL
A NATION'S IDEALS BY
THEIR ADVERTISEMENTS
—NORMAN DOUGLAS**

Rating: 1   2   3   4   5   Date Used:

134.   **NO MAN CAN RESOLVE
HIMSELF INTO HEAVEN
—D. L. MOODY**

Rating: 1   2   3   4   5   Date Used:

135.   **THE HOLY SCRIPTURES**
                       ARE OUR LETTERS
                       FROM HOME
                       —AUGUSTINE

Rating: 1   2   3   4   5   Date Used:

136.   **PEACE IS LIBERTY IN**
                       TRANQUILITY
                       —CICERO

Rating: 1   2   3   4   5   Date Used:

137.   **KEEP YOUR FACE TO**
                       THE SUNSHINE AND
                       YOU WILL NEVER SEE
                       SHADOWS—H. KELLER

Rating: 1   2   3   4   5   Date Used:

138.   **IT IS NOT WELL FOR**
                       MAN TO PRAY CREAM
                       AND LIVE SKIM MILK
                       —H. W. BEECHER

Rating: 1   2   3   4   5   Date Used:

139.   **THE LOWEST EBB IS**
                       THE TURN OF THE TIDE
                       —LONGFELLOW

Rating: 1   2   3   4   5   Date Used:

140.   **COME MY FRIENDS**
                       IT'S NOT TOO LATE TO
                       SEEK A NEWER WORLD
                       —ALFRED TENNYSON

Rating: 1   2   3   4   5   Date Used:

141.

**WHAT I BELIEVE
ABOUT GOD IS THE MOST
IMPORTANT THING
ABOUT ME—A. W. TOZER**

Rating: 1   2   3   4   5   Date Used:

142.

**TOUGH TIMES
DON'T LAST—
TOUGH PEOPLE DO
—ROBERT SCHULLER**

Rating: 1   2   3   4   5   Date Used:

143.

**IF YOU WANT THE
RAINBOW YOU GOTTA
PUT UP WITH THE RAIN
—DOLLY PARTON**

Rating: 1   2   3   4   5   Date Used:

144.

**WHEN TWO ELEPHANTS
FIGHT IT'S THE GRASS
THAT SUFFERS
—AFRICAN PROVERB**

Rating: 1   2   3   4   5   Date Used:

145.

**HE THAT CAN HAVE
PATIENCE CAN HAVE
WHAT HE WILL
—BEN FRANKLIN**

Rating: 1   2   3   4   5   Date Used:

146.

**TO SUCCEED IN
ANYTHING YOU MUST
GIVE EVERYTHING
—VINCE LOMBARDI**

Rating: 1   2   3   4   5   Date Used:

147.

**THE GROUND IS LEVEL
AT THE FOOT
OF THE CROSS
—BILLY GRAHAM**

Rating: 1   2   3   4   5   Date Used:

148.

**THE ONLY WAY TO
ACHIEVE HAPPINESS
IS NOT TO SEEK IT
—JOHN STUART MILL**

Rating: 1   2   3   4   5   Date Used:

149.

**HEALTH DEPENDS IN
LARGE MEASURE ON THE
THOUGHTS OF OUR MINDS
—MARTIN LUTHER**

Rating: 1   2   3   4   5   Date Used:

150.

**FRIENDSHIP IS GOD'S
SPECIAL WAY OF
LOVING US THROUGH
SOMEONE ELSE**

Rating: 1   2   3   4   5   Date Used:

151.

**FAITH IS FORGED
THROUGH DOUBT**

Rating: 1   2   3   4   5   Date Used:

152.

**LIVE LIFE RIGHT
AND YOU WON'T
BE LEFT**

Rating: 1   2   3   4   5   Date Used:

153.

ENJOY LIFE!
GOD INVENTED IT

Rating: 1   2   3   4   5   Date Used:

154.

OF ALL THE THINGS
YOU WEAR YOUR
EXPRESSION IS THE
MOST IMPORTANT

Rating: 1   2   3   4   5   Date Used:

155.

WHEN WE FORGIVE
WE SET OURSELVES FREE

Rating: 1   2   3   4   5   Date Used:

156.

HAPPINESS IS WITHIN
—REJOICE BY
CHOOSING JESUS

Rating: 1   2   3   4   5   Date Used:

157.

GOD WILL SURVIVE
YOUR REJECTION
—BUT YOU WON'T

Rating: 1   2   3   4   5   Date Used:

158.

TRY SOME OF THESE
FOUR-LETTER WORDS—
LOVE, HELP, GIVE, CARE

Rating: 1   2   3   4   5   Date Used:

159.

WORRY WILL NOT EMPTY
TOMORROW OF TROUBLE
BUT IT WILL ROB
TODAY OF JOY

Rating: 1   2   3   4   5   Date Used:

160.

HALF THE THINGS PEOPLE WORRY ABOUT NEVER HAPPEN

Rating: 1   2   3   4   5   Date Used:

161.

WORRY IS IRREVERENT —GOD WILL PROVIDE

Rating: 1   2   3   4   5   Date Used:

162.

IN EVERY FAILURE GOD PLANTS A SEED OF SUCCESS

Rating: 1   2   3   4   5   Date Used:

163.

GLEAN WISDOM FROM FAILURE THEN BURY THE MEMORY

Rating: 1   2   3   4   5   Date Used:

164.

TRUE HUMILITY IS A SIGN OF TRUE GREATNESS

Rating: 1   2   3   4   5   Date Used:

165.

THE COMPANY YOU KEEP DETERMINES THE TROUBLE YOU MEET

Rating: 1   2   3   4   5   Date Used:

166.

DON'T COUNT YEARS —MAKE YEARS COUNT

Rating: 1   2   3   4   5   Date Used:

167.

**IN THE WORST
STORMS WE LEARN
WHICH TREES
WILL STAND**

Rating: 1 2 3 4 5   Date Used:

168.

**ONLY HARD STORMS
SHOW WHICH TREES
ARE ALIVE AND
DEEPLY ROOTED**

Rating: 1 2 3 4 5   Date Used:

169.

**THE SON CAN WARM
YOU FOREVER**

Rating: 1 2 3 4 5   Date Used:

170.

**IN GOD WE TRUST
IS RIGHT ON
THE MONEY**

Rating: 1 2 3 4 5   Date Used:

171.

**GOD CARED ENOUGH
TO SEND HIS VERY BEST**

Rating: 1 2 3 4 5   Date Used:

172.

**TGIF
—THANK GOD
I'M FORGIVEN**

Rating: 1 2 3 4 5   Date Used:

173.

WWYD—
WHAT WILL YOU DO
WITH JESUS?

Rating: 1   2   3   4   5   Date Used:

174.

GIVE SIN AN INCH
AND YOU WILL
HAVE TO RETAKE
A MILE

Rating: 1   2   3   4   5   Date Used:

175.

TO BE OR NOT TO BE
SAVED—THAT IS THE
CRITICAL QUESTION

Rating: 1   2   3   4   5   Date Used:

176.

MARRIAGES WOULD
NOT FAIL IF THOSE
WHO SAID "I DO" DID

Rating: 1   2   3   4   5   Date Used:

177.

IF THE GRASS LOOKS
GREENER
ON THE OTHER SIDE
FERTILIZE YOURS

Rating: 1   2   3   4   5   Date Used:

178.

NOTHING DRIVES
PEOPLE TO PRAYER
LIKE PARENTING

Rating: 1   2   3   4   5   Date Used:

179.

A FAMILY THAT PRAYS TOGETHER STILL STAYS TOGETHER

Rating: 1   2   3   4   5   Date Used:

180.

GOD'S PRAYER LINE IS ALWAYS OPEN AND ALWAYS TOLL FREE

Rating: 1   2   3   4   5   Date Used:

181.

GOD'S HOME PAGE IS STILL ONLY A PRAYER AWAY

Rating: 1   2   3   4   5   Date Used:

182.

PRAY AND YOU WON'T BECOME PREY

Rating: 1   2   3   4   5   Date Used:

183.

PRAYING WILL GIVE YOU A CALM-PLEX

Rating: 1   2   3   4   5   Date Used:

184.

WORRY NOT WHO YOU ARE BUT WHOSE YOU ARE

Rating: 1   2   3   4   5   Date Used:

185.

WE WELCOME YOU WITH OPEN PSALMS

Rating: 1   2   3   4   5   Date Used:

186.

IS LIFE A PUZZLE?
WE HAVE THE MISSING
PEACE

Rating: 1   2   3   4   5   Date Used:

187.

PART-TIME FAITH
LIKE PART-TIME JOBS
CAN'T SUPPORT YOU

Rating: 1   2   3   4   5   Date Used:

188.

WHAT YOU BELIEVE
DOES MAKE A DIFFERENCE

Rating: 1   2   3   4   5   Date Used:

189.

WOULD THE EVIDENCE
CONVINCE A JURY
THAT YOU ARE
A CHRISTIAN?

Rating: 1   2   3   4   5   Date Used:

190.

THE BREAD OF LIFE
CURES SOUL HUNGER

Rating: 1   2   3   4   5   Date Used:

191.

BOOKS INFORM BUT
ONLY THE BIBLE
TRANSFORMS

Rating: 1   2   3   4   5   Date Used:

192.

MAKING A LIVING
AND MAKING A LIFE
ARE NOT THE SAME
GET A LIFE!

Rating: 1   2   3   4   5   Date Used:

193.   **LOVE IN DEED IS
LOVE INDEED**

Rating: 1   2   3   4   5   Date Used:

194.   **WHAT ON EARTH
ARE YOU DOING
FOR HEAVEN'S SAKE?**

Rating: 1   2   3   4   5   Date Used:

195.   **DON'T RUN
WITH THE WORLD
WALK WITH GOD**

Rating: 1   2   3   4   5   Date Used:

196.   **TO STAY OUT OF DEBT
ACT YOUR WAGE**

Rating: 1   2   3   4   5   Date Used:

197.   **THE BEST VITAMIN
FOR HAVING A FRIEND
IS B1**

Rating: 1   2   3   4   5   Date Used:

198.   **YOU DON'T NEED CREDIT
TO BORROW TROUBLE**

Rating: 1   2   3   4   5   Date Used:

199.   **INTELLIGENT DESIGN
IS MORE BELIEVABLE
THAN EVOLUTIONARY
ACCIDENT**

Rating: 1   2   3   4   5   Date Used:

200.

FAITH IS LIKE LOVE —IF WE HOARD IT IT SHRIVELS

Rating: 1   2   3   4   5   Date Used:

201.

IT IS BETTER NOT TO HAVE LIVED THAN NOT TO HAVE LOVED

Rating: 1   2   3   4   5   Date Used:

202.

TRYING AND FAILING IS BETTER THAN DOING NOTHING AND SUCCEEDING

Rating: 1   2   3   4   5   Date Used:

203.

WHEN YOU LOSE DON'T LOSE THE LESSON YOU HAVE LEARNED

Rating: 1   2   3   4   5   Date Used:

204.

EVOLUTION LOOKS AT OLD BONES AS GOD MAKES NEW MEN AND WOMEN

Rating: 1   2   3   4   5   Date Used:

205.

AS TRUTH STRETCHES TRUST BREAKS

Rating: 1   2   3   4   5   Date Used:

206.

BE KIND
FOR EVERYONE
YOU MEET IS PART
OF A GREAT BATTLE

Rating:　　　1　2　3　4　5　　　Date Used:

207.

ANGER IS A WIND
THAT BLOWS OUT
THE LAMP OF THE MIND

Rating:　　　1　2　3　4　5　　　Date Used:

208.

GOD OFFERS FREEDOM
FROM GUILT,
JUDGMENT, AND
SELF-CONDEMNATION

Rating:　　　1　2　3　4　5　　　Date Used:

209.

GOD LACKS NOTHING
AND IS LIMITED
BY NOTHING

Rating:　　　1　2　3　4　5　　　Date Used:

210.

OBEYING GOD IS NOT
THE EASIEST THING
BUT IT IS THE WISEST

Rating:　　　1　2　3　4　5　　　Date Used:

211.

OBEDIENCE IS THE
WAY TO EXPERIENCE
GOD'S GREATEST
BLESSING

Rating:　　　1　2　3　4　5　　　Date Used:

212.

**KEEP YOUR WORDS
SOFT AND SWEET
IN CASE YOU HAVE
TO EAT THEM**

Rating: 1   2   3   4   5   Date Used:

213.

**WHEN DREAMS
TURN TO DUST
VACUUM**

Rating: 1   2   3   4   5   Date Used:

214.

**LITTLE IS MUCH
IN THE HANDS
OF GOD**

Rating: 1   2   3   4   5   Date Used:

215.

**THERE'S NO HIGH
LIKE THE MOST HIGH**

Rating: 1   2   3   4   5   Date Used:

216.

**THE WILL OF GOD
WILL NOT TAKE YOU
WHERE HIS HAND
WILL NOT SUSTAIN YOU**

Rating: 1   2   3   4   5   Date Used:

217.

**THERE IS ONLY ONE
ULTIMATE FORCE
IN THE WORLD—GOD**

Rating: 1   2   3   4   5   Date Used:

218.

**A VERY SHORT STEP
SEPARATES IDOLATRY
FROM IMMORALITY**

Rating: 1   2   3   4   5   Date Used:

219.

**NO ONE SHOULD
DISREGARD A
RELIGION THAT CAN
MAKE BAD MEN GOOD**

Rating: 1   2   3   4   5   Date Used:

220.

**THE BIBLE IS GOD'S
PERSONAL LETTER
TO YOU**

Rating: 1   2   3   4   5   Date Used:

221.

**ALL THAT IS NEEDED
FOR EVIL TO WIN
IS FOR GOOD PEOPLE
TO DO NOTHING**

Rating: 1   2   3   4   5   Date Used:

222.

**GOD NEVER SHUTS
ONE DOOR BEFORE
HE OPENS ANOTHER**

Rating: 1   2   3   4   5   Date Used:

223.

**OUR ROAD HAS
A HOPELESS END
UNLESS WE FOLLOW
AN ENDLESS HOPE**

Rating: 1   2   3   4   5   Date Used:

224.

**IF SATAN IS A COMMA
IN LIFE DO NOT LET HIM
BE THE PERIOD**

Rating: 1   2   3   4   5   Date Used:

225.

**SPACIOUS GOALS
ALLOW PLENTY
OF ROOM TO RUN**

Rating: 1   2   3   4   5   Date Used:

226.

**BRING SONLIGHT
TO OTHERS AND YOU
WILL BE WARMED**

Rating: 1   2   3   4   5   Date Used:

227.

**IN GREAT ATTEMPTS
IT IS GLORIOUS
EVEN TO FAIL**

Rating: 1   2   3   4   5   Date Used:

228.

**WITHOUT STRUGGLE
CHARACTER
LIES DORMANT**

Rating: 1   2   3   4   5   Date Used:

229.

**GENIUS IS THE ABILITY
TO MAKE THE
COMPLEX SIMPLE**

Rating: 1   2   3   4   5   Date Used:

230.

**ONE GREAT ENEMY
OF TRUTH IS THE PERSISTENT
PERSUASIVE MYTH**

Rating: 1   2   3   4   5   Date Used:

231.

**THINGS WILL GET
BETTER DESPITE
OUR EFFORTS TO
IMPROVE THEM**

Rating: 1   2   3   4   5   Date Used:

232.

**SMALL OPPORTUNITIES
ARE OFTEN THE
BEGINNING OF
GREAT ENTERPRISES**

Rating: 1   2   3   4   5   Date Used:

233.

**EVERY JOB IS THE
SELF-PORTRAIT OF
THE ONE WHO DID IT**

Rating: 1   2   3   4   5   Date Used:

234.

**THE TRULY GREAT
KNOW THE SECRET
OF SERVANTHOOD**

Rating: 1   2   3   4   5   Date Used:

235.

**WHEN TRUTH BECOMES
RELATIVE ALL THINGS
BECOME DOUBTFUL**

Rating: 1   2   3   4   5   Date Used:

236.

**IT IS IN SEEKING
HAPPINESS FOR
OTHERS THAT WE
FIND IT OURSELVES**

Rating: 1   2   3   4   5   Date Used:

237.

**SUCCESS IS SIMPLY
A MATTER OF LUCK
—ASK ANY FAILURE**

Rating: 1 2 3 4 5   Date Used:

238.

**A MAN WHO FALLS IS A
FAILURE ONLY WHEN
HE SAYS SOMEONE
PUSHED HIM**

Rating: 1 2 3 4 5   Date Used:

239.

**STRETCH THE MIND
WITH A NEW IDEA
AND IT'S NEVER THE
SAME SIZE AGAIN**

Rating: 1 2 3 4 5   Date Used:

240.

**THERE CAN BE NO
COURAGE WITHOUT
FEAR AND RISK**

Rating: 1 2 3 4 5   Date Used:

241.

**SOME FAILURES
THINK AND DO NOT
OTHER FAILURES
DO AND THINK NOT**

Rating: 1 2 3 4 5   Date Used:

242.

**SOME DREAM OF
ACCOMPLISHMENTS
WHILE OTHERS WAKE
AND DO THEM**

Rating: 1 2 3 4 5   Date Used:

243.

GOD GIVES THE SHOULDER TO FIT THE BURDEN

Rating: 1   2   3   4   5   Date Used:

244.

WHEN GOD PARDONS HE CONSIGNS THE OFFENSE TO ETERNAL FORGETFULNESS

Rating: 1   2   3   4   5   Date Used:

245.

ONE WHO LACKS THE COURAGE TO START IS ALREADY FINISHED

Rating: 1   2   3   4   5   Date Used:

246.

GOD INTERVENED IN HUMAN AFFAIRS AT THE CROSSROADS OF HISTORY

Rating: 1   2   3   4   5   Date Used:

247.

WE CAN ONLY FULLY SEE GOD'S GRACE FROM THE FOOT OF THE CROSS

Rating: 1   2   3   4   5   Date Used:

248.

PERSEVERE— EVEN THE SNAILS REACHED THE ARK

Rating: 1   2   3   4   5   Date Used:

249.

**FAILURE TO FORGIVE
DESTROYS ONE'S
OWN LINK TO
FORGIVENESS**

Rating: 1   2   3   4   5   Date Used:

250.

**DEFENDING TRUTH
WITH TIMIDITY
IS COWARDICE**

Rating: 1   2   3   4   5   Date Used:

251.

**THE MIND FORGETS
BUT THE HEART
REMEMBERS**

Rating: 1   2   3   4   5   Date Used:

252.

**A SMILE IS A GIFT
WE CAN BESTOW
ON OTHERS**

Rating: 1   2   3   4   5   Date Used:

253.

**FRIENDS
MULTIPLY JOY AND
DIVIDE SORROW**

Rating: 1   2   3   4   5   Date Used:

254.

**GOD IS NOT
DISILLUSIONED BY US
—HE NEVER HAD
ANY ILLUSIONS**

Rating: 1   2   3   4   5   Date Used:

255.

**NOT SURE WHY YOU
ARE HERE OR
WHERE YOU ARE
GOING? YOU'RE LOST**

Rating: 1 2 3 4 5   Date Used:

256.

**THE JOB OF THE
CHRISTIAN IS NOT
TO BE LIKED BUT
TO BE OBEDIENT**

Rating: 1 2 3 4 5   Date Used:

257.

**RATHER FAIL WITH
HONOR THAN
SUCCEED WITH FRAUD
—SOPHOCLES**

Rating: 1 2 3 4 5   Date Used:

258.

**YOU CAN OBSERVE
A LOT JUST BY
WATCHING
—YOGI BERRA**

Rating: 1 2 3 4 5   Date Used:

259.

**IT IS BETTER
TO PREVENT
THAN TO CURE
—PERUVIAN PROVERB**

Rating: 1 2 3 4 5   Date Used:

260.

**BEFORE GOD CAN
DELIVER US WE MUST
UNDECEIVE OURSELVES
—AUGUSTINE**

Rating: 1 2 3 4 5   Date Used:

261.

**NOTHING IS MORE
HARMFUL TO A NEW
TRUTH THAN AN OLD
ERROR—GOETHE**

Rating: 1   2   3   4   5   Date Used:

262.

**WHATEVER YOU LOVE
MORE THAN GOD
IS YOUR IDOL
—D. L. MOODY**

Rating: 1   2   3   4   5   Date Used:

263.

**PRAYER IS THE
PRACTICE OF DRAWING
ON THE GRACE OF GOD
—OSWALD CHAMBERS**

Rating: 1   2   3   4   5   Date Used:

264.

**FAILING TO PREPARE
IS PREPARING TO FAIL
—JOHN WOODEN**

Rating: 1   2   3   4   5   Date Used:

265.

**GODLINESS TETHERS
SELF-INTEREST AND
FEEDS CHARACTER
—VOLTAIRE**

Rating: 1   2   3   4   5   Date Used:

266.

**TAKING AWAY GOD
EVEN IN THOUGHT
DISSOLVES ALL
—JOHN LOCKE**

Rating: 1   2   3   4   5   Date Used:

267.
AMERICA YOU MUST
BE BORN AGAIN
—MARTIN L. KING JR.

Rating: 1   2   3   4   5   Date Used:

268.
HATE IMPRISONS
LOVE FREES
—RUBIN CARTER

Rating: 1   2   3   4   5   Date Used:

269.
A PEOPLE THAT VALUES
PRIVILEGE ABOVE
PRINCIPLE SOON LOSES
BOTH—D. EISENHOWER

Rating: 1   2   3   4   5   Date Used:

270.
WHAT THOU WILT
WHEN THOU WILT
HOW THOU WILT
—JOHN NEWTON

Rating: 1   2   3   4   5   Date Used:

271.
THERE IS A GOD-SHAPED
VACUUM IN EVERY
HEART—PASCAL

Rating: 1   2   3   4   5   Date Used:

272.
AN INFINITE GOD CAN
GIVE ALL OF HIMSELF
TO EACH OF HIS
CHILDREN—A. W. TOZER

Rating: 1   2   3   4   5   Date Used:

273.

**OUR VOCATION TO BE
BEAUTIFUL MUST BE
FULL OF THOUGHT FOR
OTHERS—MOTHER TERESA**

Rating: 1 2 3 4 5   Date Used:

274.

**IF THINGS ARE WELL
IN A NATION'S HOMES
THINGS WILL BE WELL
IN THE NATION**

Rating: 1 2 3 4 5   Date Used:

275.

**HOW THE BEST TREAT
THE LEAST MAY
DETERMINE WHAT
HAPPENS TO THE REST**

Rating: 1 2 3 4 5   Date Used:

276.

**IN GOD'S EXCHANGE
YOU ARE WORTH
FAR MORE THAN
YOU CAN IMAGINE**

Rating: 1 2 3 4 5   Date Used:

277.

**YOU CAN'T BUILD
UP AND OUT UNTIL
YOU DIG DEEP WITHIN**

Rating: 1 2 3 4 5   Date Used:

278.

**IF YOU'RE ON CLOUD 3
VISIT US—
WE CAN PUT YOU
ON CLOUD 9**

Rating: 1 2 3 4 5   Date Used:

279.
HE WHO LAUGHS
LASTS

Rating: 1   2   3   4   5   Date Used:

280.
VOLUNTEERS BELIEVE
IN ALL WORK
AND NO PAY

Rating: 1   2   3   4   5   Date Used:

281.
IF YOU SCATTER
THORNS
DON'T GO BAREFOOT

Rating: 1   2   3   4   5   Date Used:

282.
THE MOST HANDICAPPED
WORKER IN THE WORLD
IS A
NEGATIVE THINKER

Rating: 1   2   3   4   5   Date Used:

283.
TODAY IS A GIFT
FROM GOD—
USE IT WISELY

Rating: 1   2   3   4   5   Date Used:

284.
WARNING: HUMOR
MAY BE HAZARDOUS
TO YOUR ILLNESS

Rating: 1   2   3   4   5   Date Used:

285.
WE WILL HELP YOU
STUDY FOR THE
FINAL FINAL EXAM

Rating: 1   2   3   4   5   Date Used:

286.   **LIFE ALTERATION
                             CAN START AT
                             OUR ALTAR**

Rating: 1   2   3   4   5   Date Used:

287.   **WE PRAY—
                             BUT ONLY ON DAYS
                              OF THE WEEK
                              ENDING IN Y**

Rating: 1   2   3   4   5   Date Used:

288.   **THE BIBLE
                             ISN'T OUTDATED
                             —IT IS ETERNAL**

Rating: 1   2   3   4   5   Date Used:

289.   **WE LIE MOST LOUDLY
                              WHEN WE LIE
                              TO OURSELVES**

Rating: 1   2   3   4   5   Date Used:

290.   **NO LEAPS OF FAITH
                             NEEDED TO JUMP
                             FROM GOD'S WORD
                              INTO TOMORROW**

Rating: 1   2   3   4   5   Date Used:

291.   **DOWNLOAD A NEW
                             OPERATING PROGRAM
                              GET ON-LINE
                              WITH GOD**

Rating: 1   2   3   4   5   Date Used:

292.

WE HAVE
A TRUST DEPARTMENT
YOU CAN BANK ON

Rating: 1   2   3   4   5   Date Used:

293.

NOTHING IS SWEETER
THAN ONE OF OUR
SUNDAYS

Rating: 1   2   3   4   5   Date Used:

294.

THERE'S PARDON FOR
TRANSGRESSIONS PAST
IT MATTERS NOT
HOW DARK THE CAST

Rating: 1   2   3   4   5   Date Used:

295.

TO BE A CHRISTIAN
IS TO BE REBORN—
FREE—UNAFRAID—AND
IMMORTALLY YOUNG

Rating: 1   2   3   4   5   Date Used:

296.

WE ARE TOO BLESSED
TO BE STRESSED
OR DEPRESSED

Rating: 1   2   3   4   5   Date Used:

297.

DESPOTISM MAY DO
WITHOUT FAITH BUT
FREEDOM CANNOT
—DE TOCQUEVILLE

Rating: 1   2   3   4   5   Date Used:

298.

**YOU WON'T FIND FAULT
IF YOUR EYES
ARE ON JESUS**

Rating: 1   2   3   4   5   Date Used:

299.

**WEALTH IS NOT
WHAT YOU HAVE
BUT WHO YOU HAVE**

Rating: 1   2   3   4   5   Date Used:

300.

**IF YOU WANT TO BE
RICH—BECOME
AN HEIR TO
THE KING OF KINGS**

Rating: 1   2   3   4   5   Date Used:

301.

**SUCCESS IS
99 PERCENT
FAILURE**

Rating: 1   2   3   4   5   Date Used:

302.

**THOSE WHO CAN'T
LAUGH AT THEMSELVES
LEAVE THE JOB
TO OTHERS**

Rating: 1   2   3   4   5   Date Used:

303.

**ONLY BY THE
LIGHT OF GOD
DO WE KNOW
WHAT HAS VALUE**

Rating: 1   2   3   4   5   Date Used:

304.

**IF YOU WANT YOUR
DREAMS TO COME TRUE
DON'T OVERSLEEP**

Rating: 1   2   3   4   5   Date Used:

305.

**IDEAS ARE A DIME A
DOZEN—PEOPLE WHO
CAN MAKE THEM REALITY
ARE PRICELESS**

Rating: 1   2   3   4   5   Date Used:

306.

**BE SO STRONG THAT
NOTHING CAN DISTURB
YOUR PEACE OF MIND**

Rating: 1   2   3   4   5   Date Used:

307.

**BE TOO BIG FOR WORRY
AND TOO NOBLE
FOR ANGER**

Rating: 1   2   3   4   5   Date Used:

308.

**WHEN SATAN KNOCKS
AT YOUR DOOR ASK
JESUS TO ANSWER IT**

Rating: 1   2   3   4   5   Date Used:

309.

**DON'T EXPECT A
MILLION-DOLLAR
ANSWER TO A
TEN-CENT PRAYER**

Rating: 1   2   3   4   5   Date Used:

310.

NEPOTISM IS A MATTER OF PUTTING ON HEIRS

Rating: 1   2   3   4   5   Date Used:

311.

RACISM HAS HIGH INTEREST HATES

Rating: 1   2   3   4   5   Date Used:

312.

A GENIUS IS A PERSON WHO AIMS AT WHAT NO ONE ELSE CAN SEE —AND HITS IT

Rating: 1   2   3   4   5   Date Used:

313.

EXPERIENCE IS KNOWING A LOT OF THINGS YOU SHOULDN'T DO

Rating: 1   2   3   4   5   Date Used:

314.

EDUCATION IS A PROGRESSIVE DISCOVERY OF OUR OWN IGNORANCE

Rating: 1   2   3   4   5   Date Used:

315.

THERE IS NO EVIDENCE THAT THE TONGUE IS ATTACHED TO THE BRAIN

Rating: 1   2   3   4   5   Date Used:

316.

NOTHING IS IMPOSSIBLE
UNTIL IT IS SENT
TO A COMMITTEE

Rating: 1   2   3   4   5   Date Used:

317.

WHEN WE FAIL TO
LISTEN TO GOD WE
MISS HIS BLESSING

Rating: 1   2   3   4   5   Date Used:

318.

DON'T WAIT FOR YOUR
SHIP TO COME IN
—SWIM OUT TO IT

Rating: 1   2   3   4   5   Date Used:

319.

MAKE THE MISTAKES
OF YESTERDAY
YOUR LESSONS
OF TODAY

Rating: 1   2   3   4   5   Date Used:

320.

A PERSON'S DREAMS
ARE AN INDEX
TO GREATNESS

Rating: 1   2   3   4   5   Date Used:

321.

A PERSON WITHOUT
A PURPOSE IS LIKE
A SHIP WITHOUT
A RUDDER

Rating: 1   2   3   4   5   Date Used:

322.

**THE BEST WAY TO
CHEER YOURSELF
IS TO CHEER UP
SOMEONE ELSE**

Rating: 1   2   3   4   5   Date Used:

323.

**FAILURE IS THE
OPPORTUNITY TO
BEGIN BETTER**

Rating: 1   2   3   4   5   Date Used:

324.

**WORRY IS
THE MISUSE
OF IMAGINATION**

Rating: 1   2   3   4   5   Date Used:

325.

**STRIVE TO LIVE SO
THAT WHEN YOU DIE
EVEN THE UNDERTAKER
WILL BE UNHAPPY**

Rating: 1   2   3   4   5   Date Used:

326.

**ABOUT THE ONLY
THING THAT COMES
WITHOUT EFFORT
IS OLD AGE**

Rating: 1   2   3   4   5   Date Used:

327.

**SUCCESS IS A
JOURNEY—NOT
A DESTINATION**

Rating: 1   2   3   4   5   Date Used:

328. **LET EACH DAY BE
A MASTERPIECE**

Rating: 1 2 3 4 5 Date Used:

329. **SATAN WANTS
TO CONTROL YOU
GOD WANTS
TO LEAD YOU**

Rating: 1 2 3 4 5 Date Used:

330. **MOST OF LIFE'S
SIGNIFICANT BATTLES
ARE WAGED WITHIN**

Rating: 1 2 3 4 5 Date Used:

331. **IT'S NOT YOUR
POSITION THAT
COUNTS—IT'S
YOUR DISPOSITION**

Rating: 1 2 3 4 5 Date Used:

332. **IN TIMES LIKE THESE
REMEMBER THAT
WE'VE ALWAYS HAD
TIMES LIKE THESE**

Rating: 1 2 3 4 5 Date Used:

333. **PEOPLE RARELY
SUCCEED AT ANYTHING
UNLESS THEY HAVE
FUN DOING IT**

Rating: 1 2 3 4 5 Date Used:

334.

**SUCCESS SEEMS TO
BE A MATTER OF
HANGING ON AFTER
OTHERS LET GO**

Rating: 1   2   3   4   5   Date Used:

335.

**PATIENCE IS BITTER
BUT ITS FRUIT
IS VERY SWEET**

Rating: 1   2   3   4   5   Date Used:

336.

**CRITICISM IS AN
INDIRECT FORM
OF BOASTING**

Rating: 1   2   3   4   5   Date Used:

337.

**IF BETTER
IS POSSIBLE
THEN GOOD
IS NOT ENOUGH**

Rating: 1   2   3   4   5   Date Used:

338.

**HATRED IS
LOVE WITHOUT
THE FACTS**

Rating: 1   2   3   4   5   Date Used:

339.

**WASTE NOT
FRESH TEARS
OVER OLD GRIEFS**

Rating: 1   2   3   4   5   Date Used:

340.

THE REAL MEASURE
OF ANY PERSON
IS THE SIZE
OF THEIR HEART

Rating: 1   2   3   4   5   Date Used:

341.

ONCE YOU HAVE
LEARNED TO LOVE
YOU HAVE
LEARNED TO LIVE

Rating: 1   2   3   4   5   Date Used:

342.

DEAR GOD—
MAKE ME AS GOOD
AS MY DOG
THINKS I AM

Rating: 1   2   3   4   5   Date Used:

343.

A GREAT MARRIAGE
REQUIRES
A BLIND WIFE
AND A DEAF HUSBAND

Rating: 1   2   3   4   5   Date Used:

344.

GOD SENDS US FLOWERS
EVERY SPRING AND A
SUNRISE AND SUNSET
EVERY DAY

Rating: 1   2   3   4   5   Date Used:

345.

WHEN YOU WANT TO
TALK HE'LL LISTEN

Rating: 1   2   3   4   5   Date Used:

346.

**WORK DONE WITH
LITTLE EFFORT IS
LIKELY TO YIELD
LITTLE RESULT**

Rating: 1   2   3   4   5   Date Used:

347.

**GOOD WITHOUT
GOD EQUALS
0**

Rating: 1   2   3   4   5   Date Used:

348.

**CONSCIENCE IS
A FAULTS ALARM**

Rating: 1   2   3   4   5   Date Used:

349.

**HOTHEADS
NEVER SET
THE WORLD ON FIRE**

Rating: 1   2   3   4   5   Date Used:

350.

**GOD DOESN'T ASK ABOUT
OUR CAPABILITY—JUST
OUR AVAILABILITY**

Rating: 1   2   3   4   5   Date Used:

351.

**WHO SAVES?
JESUS
AND THAT'S OUR
FINAL ANSWER**

Rating: 1   2   3   4   5   Date Used:

352.   **SIN CAUSES
THE CUP OF JOY
TO SPRING A LEAK**

Rating: 1   2   3   4   5   Date Used:

353.   **THE CORRUPT SOUL
INFECTS ALL IN ITS
NEIGHBORHOOD**

Rating: 1   2   3   4   5   Date Used:

354.   **IF YOU WANT
TO BE SUCCESSFUL
LEARN TO BE
PERSISTENT**

Rating: 1   2   3   4   5   Date Used:

355.   **JESUS CHRIST
HAS BROUGHT
LIFE TO LIGHT
AND LIGHT TO LIFE**

Rating: 1   2   3   4   5   Date Used:

356.   **THE HOLY SPIRIT
MAKES GOD'S WORDS
PERSONAL**

Rating: 1   2   3   4   5   Date Used:

357.   **YOU CAN ONLY
GAIN VICTORY
BY SURRENDER
TO JESUS CHRIST**

Rating: 1   2   3   4   5   Date Used:

358.

WHERE THERE IS
NO GOD
THERE IS
NO HUMANITY

Rating: 1 2 3 4 5 Date Used:

359.

THE GOSPEL
WASN'T GIVEN TO
AN AD AGENCY —
IT CAME TO US

Rating: 1 2 3 4 5 Date Used:

360.

THOSE WHO KNEEL
BEFORE GOD
CAN STAND
BEFORE ANYONE

Rating: 1 2 3 4 5 Date Used:

361.

TO BE ALMOST SAVED
IS TO BE
TOTALLY LOST

Rating: 1 2 3 4 5 Date Used:

362.

GIVE GOD
WHAT'S RIGHT—
NOT WHAT'S LEFT

Rating: 1 2 3 4 5 Date Used:

363.

GOD DOESN'T WANT
A SHARE OF LIFE
—HE WANTS
WHOLE OWNERSHIP

Rating: 1 2 3 4 5 Date Used:

364.   **IF YOU HAVE
TRUTH DECAY
BRUSH UP
ON THE BIBLE**

Rating: 1   2   3   4   5   Date Used:

365.   **KINDNESS IS HARD
TO GIVE AWAY
BECAUSE IT KEEPS
COMING BACK**

Rating: 1   2   3   4   5   Date Used:

366.   **STRENGTH COMES
FROM STRUGGLE
WEAKNESS COMES
FROM EASE**

Rating: 1   2   3   4   5   Date Used:

367.   **EXPOSURE TO THE
SON PREVENTS
BURNING**

Rating: 1   2   3   4   5   Date Used:

368.   **EVANGELISM IS NOT
AN OPTION FOR THE
CHRISTIAN LIFE
—LUIS PALAU**

Rating: 1   2   3   4   5   Date Used:

369.   **DO GOOD WITH WHAT
THOU HAST, OR IT WILL
DO THEE NO GOOD
—WILLIAM PENN**

Rating: 1   2   3   4   5   Date Used:

370. **GREAT IS TRUTH
AND SHALL
PREVAIL
—T. BROOKS**

Rating: 1 2 3 4 5 Date Used:

371. **UNDERSTANDING IS
THE REWARD OF FAITH
—AUGUSTINE**

Rating: 1 2 3 4 5 Date Used:

372. **IT IS THE END
THAT CROWNS US
NOT THE FIGHT
—R. HERRICK**

Rating: 1 2 3 4 5 Date Used:

373. **A FAITH THAT HASN'T
BEEN TESTED CAN'T BE
TRUSTED—A. ROGERS**

Rating: 1 2 3 4 5 Date Used:

374. **FAITH IS A LIVING,
DARING CONFIDENCE
IN GOD'S GRACE
—MARTIN LUTHER**

Rating: 1 2 3 4 5 Date Used:

375. **UNLESS HE WANTED
YOU—YOU WOULD NOT
BE WANTING HIM
—C. S. LEWIS**

Rating: 1 2 3 4 5 Date Used:

376.

**OUR OPPORTUNITIES
TO DO GOOD
ARE OUR TALENTS
—COTTON MATHER**

Rating: 1 2 3 4 5 Date Used:

377.

**IT IS IMPOSSIBLE TO
ENSLAVE A BIBLE-
READING PEOPLE
—HORACE GREELEY**

Rating: 1 2 3 4 5 Date Used:

378.

**YOU CAN'T HOLD
A MAN DOWN WITHOUT
STAYING DOWN WITH HIM
—BOOKER T. WASHINGTON**

Rating: 1 2 3 4 5 Date Used:

379.

**ONE LOYAL FRIEND
IS WORTH
TEN THOUSAND
RELATIVES —EURIPIDES**

Rating: 1 2 3 4 5 Date Used:

380.

**MAN PROPOSES, BUT
GOD DISPOSES
—THOMAS A KEMPIS**

Rating: 1 2 3 4 5 Date Used:

381.

**AMERICA MAY DIE
FROM THE DELUSION SHE
HAS MORAL LEADERSHIP
—WILL ROGERS**

Rating: 1 2 3 4 5 Date Used:

382.

**WHERE ONE MAN READS
THE BIBLE A HUNDRED
READ YOU AND ME
—D. L. MOODY**

Rating: 1 2 3 4 5   Date Used:

383.

**THE TRUE CHRISTIAN
IDEAL IS NOT TO BE
HAPPY BUT TO BE HOLY
—A. W. TOZER**

Rating: 1 2 3 4 5   Date Used:

384.

**MAN IS A REED—THE
WEAKEST THING IN
NATURE—BUT HE IS A
THINKING REED—PASCAL**

Rating: 1 2 3 4 5   Date Used:

385.

**REJOICE! THE LORD IS KING
YOUR LORD AND KING
ADORE—CHARLES WESLEY**

Rating: 1 2 3 4 5   Date Used:

386.

**IF YOU HAVE NO JOY
THERE'S A LEAK IN
FAITH SOMEWHERE
—H. W. BEECHER**

Rating: 1 2 3 4 5   Date Used:

387.

**HOW COME YOU ONLY
TALK TO ME WHEN
YOU'RE IN TROUBLE?
—GOD**

Rating: 1 2 3 4 5   Date Used:

388.
**WILL THE ROAD
YOU ARE ON TAKE
YOU TO MY HOUSE?
—GOD**

Rating: 1   2   3   4   5   Date Used:

389.
**WHAT IF YOU DON'T
BELIEVE IN ME AND
YOU'RE WRONG?
—GOD**

Rating: 1   2   3   4   5   Date Used:

390.
**I DON'T QUESTION
YOUR EXISTENCE
—GOD**

Rating: 1   2   3   4   5   Date Used:

391.
**IF WE DON'T TALK
YOU DON'T
HAVE A PRAYER
—GOD**

Rating: 1   2   3   4   5   Date Used:

392.
**I'M IN THE BOOK
—GOD**

Rating: 1   2   3   4   5   Date Used:

393.
**THE LAST TIME THINGS
WERE THIS MESSED UP
I SENT A FLOOD
—GOD**

Rating: 1   2   3   4   5   Date Used:

394.   **THAT EXTRA MILE**
                    IS NEVER CROWDED

Rating: 1   2   3   4   5   Date Used:

395.   **PEOPLE ARE DOWN**
                    ON THE BIBLE
                    BECAUSE THEY ARE
                    NOT UP ON IT

Rating: 1   2   3   4   5   Date Used:

396.   **ASPIRE TO INSPIRE**
                    BEFORE YOU EXPIRE

Rating: 1   2   3   4   5   Date Used:

397.   **WE CAN CONTROL**
                    OUR ACTIONS BUT
                    NOT THEIR FINAL
                    CONSEQUENCES

Rating: 1   2   3   4   5   Date Used:

398.   **LEADERS ARE ABLE**
                    TO ROCK THE BOAT
                    WITHOUT SINKING IT

Rating: 1   2   3   4   5   Date Used:

399.   **PLANT A LITTLE GOSSIP**
                    AND YOU'LL REAP A
                    HARVEST OF REGRET

Rating: 1   2   3   4   5   Date Used:

400.   **A HEART IS HAPPIEST**
                    WHEN IT BEATS
                    FOR OTHERS

Rating: 1   2   3   4   5   Date Used:

401.

MANY PARENTS DON'T RAISE CHILDREN—THEY FINANCE THEM

Rating: 1   2   3   4   5   Date Used:

402.

WHEN MEETING TEMPTATION TURN TO THE RIGHT

Rating: 1   2   3   4   5   Date Used:

403.

LIVE SO YOU WOULDN'T BE ASHAMED TO SELL YOUR PARROT TO THE TOWN GOSSIP

Rating: 1   2   3   4   5   Date Used:

404.

THE SELF-MADE MAN ALWAYS SEEMS TO ADMIRE HIS MAKER

Rating: 1   2   3   4   5   Date Used:

405.

IF YOU STRETCH THE TRUTH IT MAY SNAP BACK

Rating: 1   2   3   4   5   Date Used:

406.

MAY GOD TEACH US TO SPEAK WITH THE ACCENT OF HIS LOVE

Rating: 1   2   3   4   5   Date Used:

407.

**EVERY DAY IS
PRECIOUS—ONE
DAY WITHOUT GROWTH
IS SQUANDERED**

Rating: 1   2   3   4   5   Date Used:

408.

**EVERY ACT SHOULD
BE PERFORMED
AS IF ETERNITY
DEPENDS ON IT**

Rating: 1   2   3   4   5   Date Used:

409.

**BE NICE TO YOUR
KIDS, THEY'LL CHOOSE
YOUR NURSING HOME**

Rating: 1   2   3   4   5   Date Used:

410.

**HAPPINESS IS NOT IN
DOING WHAT YOU LIKE
BUT IN
LIKING WHAT YOU DO**

Rating: 1   2   3   4   5   Date Used:

411.

**STAYING ANGRY IS
LIKE TAKING POISON
AND WAITING FOR THE
OTHER PERSON TO DIE**

Rating: 1   2   3   4   5   Date Used:

412.

**YOU CANNOT
KILL TIME
WITHOUT INJURING
ETERNITY**

Rating: 1   2   3   4   5   Date Used:

413.

MEDITATE ON THE BIBLE AND YOU'LL FALL INTO THE HANDS OF GOD

Rating: 1 2 3 4 5 Date Used:

414.

LIFE DOESN'T GIVE MAKE-UP EXAMS

Rating: 1 2 3 4 5 Date Used:

415.

THIS CHURCH IS PRAYER-CONDITIONED

Rating: 1 2 3 4 5 Date Used:

416.

THE ACID TEST OF FAITH IS OBEDIENCE

Rating: 1 2 3 4 5 Date Used:

417.

IF YOU DRIVE WHILE YOU ARE DRUNK CARRY YOUR COFFIN IN THE TRUNK

Rating: 1 2 3 4 5 Date Used:

418.

HARDLY A FOOL IS NOW ALIVE WHO PASSED ON A HILL GOING 65

Rating: 1 2 3 4 5 Date Used:

419.   **GOD DRIVES US
TO OUR BREAKING
POINT—SO THAT
HE CAN FIX US**

Rating: 1   2   3   4   5   Date Used:

420.   **A FAMILY ALTAR
CAN ALTER
A FAMILY**

Rating: 1   2   3   4   5   Date Used:

421.   **WHEN GOD ORDAINS
HE SUSTAINS**

Rating: 1   2   3   4   5   Date Used:

422.   **HAPPINESS IN LIFE
DEPENDS ON
THE QUALITY OF
YOUR THOUGHTS**

Rating: 1   2   3   4   5   Date Used:

423.   **A JOB IS HARD
BY THE YARD
BUT A CINCH
BY THE INCH**

Rating: 1   2   3   4   5   Date Used:

424.   **SERVICE IS LOVE
IN OVERALLS**

Rating: 1   2   3   4   5   Date Used:

425.

**GOD DOESN'T CALL
THE QUALIFIED
HE QUALIFIES
THE CALLED**

Rating: 1   2   3   4   5   Date Used:

426.

**PRAY HARDEST
WHEN IT'S HARDEST
TO PRAY**

Rating: 1   2   3   4   5   Date Used:

427.

**YOUTH AND BEAUTY
FADE, CHARACTER
ENDURES FOREVER**

Rating: 1   2   3   4   5   Date Used:

428.

**YOUTH IS NOT
A TIME OF LIFE
—IT IS
A STATE OF MIND**

Rating: 1   2   3   4   5   Date Used:

429.

**YOUTH IS A GIFT
OF NATURE
BUT AGE IS
A WORK OF ART**

Rating: 1   2   3   4   5   Date Used:

430.

**MATURITY IS THE
CAPACITY TO ENDURE
UNCERTAINTY**

Rating: 1   2   3   4   5   Date Used:

431. **REMEMBERED SORROW
SWEETENS PRESENT JOY**

Rating: 1   2   3   4   5   Date Used:

432. **IF GOD
IS YOUR CO-PILOT
SWAP SEATS**

Rating: 1   2   3   4   5   Date Used:

433. **EXERCISE DAILY
—WALK WITH
THE LORD**

Rating: 1   2   3   4   5   Date Used:

434. **ALL DESIRE PEACE
BUT FEW DESIRE
THOSE THINGS THAT
MAKE FOR PEACE**

Rating: 1   2   3   4   5   Date Used:

435. **FAILING MORALLY
IS BAD—FAILING
TO REPENT IS WORSE**

Rating: 1   2   3   4   5   Date Used:

436. **THE BIBLE IS THE
BEST TV GUIDE**

Rating: 1   2   3   4   5   Date Used:

437. **AFTER ALL
IS SAID AND DONE
MORE IS OFTEN
SAID THAN DONE**

Rating: 1   2   3   4   5   Date Used:

438.

**CREATOR AND
CREATURE CAN ONLY
COME TOGETHER
AT THE CROSS**

Rating: 1   2   3   4   5   Date Used:

439.

**HUMILITY IS AN
ONGOING CHOICE
TO CREDIT GOD
FOR OUR GIFTS**

Rating: 1   2   3   4   5   Date Used:

440.

**A LOT OF KNEELING
KEEPS YOU
IN GOOD STANDING**

Rating: 1   2   3   4   5   Date Used:

441.

**BE FISHERS OF MEN—
YOU CATCH THEM
JESUS WILL CLEAN THEM**

Rating: 1   2   3   4   5   Date Used:

442.

**A COINCIDENCE IS
WHEN GOD CHOOSES
TO REMAIN
ANONYMOUS**

Rating: 1   2   3   4   5   Date Used:

443.

**GOD GRADES
ON THE CROSS—
NOT ON THE CURVE**

Rating: 1   2   3   4   5   Date Used:

444.

GOD PREFERS
FRUITS OF THE SPIRIT
TO RELIGIOUS NUTS

Rating: 1   2   3   4   5   Date Used:

445.

THE TASK IS NEVER
AS GREAT
AS THE POWER
BEHIND US

Rating: 1   2   3   4   5   Date Used:

446.

DON'T PRAY TO GIVE
GOD INSTRUCTIONS
—JUST REPORT
FOR DUTY

Rating: 1   2   3   4   5   Date Used:

447.

BE QUIET ENOUGH
TO HEAR
GOD'S WHISPERS

Rating: 1   2   3   4   5   Date Used:

448.

WE SET THE SAIL
GOD MAKES THE WIND

Rating: 1   2   3   4   5   Date Used:

449.

SATAN FATHERS LIES
GOD FATHERS TRUTH
SATAN FATHERS HATE
GOD FATHERS LOVE

Rating: 1   2   3   4   5   Date Used:

450.

**THE MORE YOU HAVE
THE MORE YOU WANT
THE LESS YOU WANT
THE MORE YOU HAVE**

Rating: 1   2   3   4   5   Date Used:

451.

**IF YOU HELP SOMEONE
ALONG THE MAIN
YOUR LIFE WILL NOT
BE LIVED IN VAIN**

Rating: 1   2   3   4   5   Date Used:

452.

**DON'T RAISE YOUR
VOICE
RAISE YOUR
REASON**

Rating: 1   2   3   4   5   Date Used:

453.

**THE GREATEST RISK
OFTEN IS NOT TO
TAKE ONE**

Rating: 1   2   3   4   5   Date Used:

454.

**WHEN THERE'S AN
EMPTINESS WITHIN
ONLY GOD
CAN FILL IT**

Rating: 1   2   3   4   5   Date Used:

455.

**CONSCIENCE TELLS YOU
WHAT'S WRONG
IT DOESN'T STOP YOU
FROM DOING IT**

Rating: 1   2   3   4   5   Date Used:

456.   **FOR EVERY SIN**
                                SATAN HAS
                                AN EXCUSE

Rating: 1   2   3   4   5   Date Used:

457.   **TROUBLES ARE THE**
                                TOOLS GOD USES
                                TO SHAPE US
                                FOR BETTER THINGS

Rating: 1   2   3   4   5   Date Used:

458.   **PRAYER PULLS US**
                                CLOSER TO THE
                                HEART OF GOD

Rating: 1   2   3   4   5   Date Used:

459.   **A SPEECH DOESN'T**
                                HAVE TO BE ETERNAL
                                TO BE IMMORTAL

Rating: 1   2   3   4   5   Date Used:

460.   **LIFE'S MOST**
                                MAGNIFICENT
                                WONDER IS
                                GOD'S MERCY

Rating: 1   2   3   4   5   Date Used:

461.   **IF GOD HAD**
                                A REFRIGERATOR
                                YOUR PICTURE
                                WOULD BE ON IT

Rating: 1   2   3   4   5   Date Used:

462. **NONE CAN BE FIT FOR
THE FUTURE LIFE WHO
HAS NOT PRACTICED IT
NOW—AUGUSTINE**

Rating: 1 2 3 4 5 Date Used:

463. **THE CHRISTIAN UNDER
TROUBLE DOESN'T
BREAK UP HE BREAKS
OUT—E. STANLEY JONES**

Rating: 1 2 3 4 5 Date Used:

464. **I KNOW THE BIBLE
IS INSPIRED BECAUSE
IT INSPIRED ME
—DWIGHT L. MOODY**

Rating: 1 2 3 4 5 Date Used:

465. **NEVER BE AFRAID TO
TRUST AN UNKNOWN
FUTURE TO A KNOWN GOD
—CORRIE TEN BOOM**

Rating: 1 2 3 4 5 Date Used:

466. **NO PERSON WAS EVER
HONORED FOR WHAT
THEY RECEIVED
—CALVIN COOLIDGE**

Rating: 1 2 3 4 5 Date Used:

467. **YOU MISS 100 PERCENT
OF THE SHOTS
YOU NEVER TAKE
—WAYNE GRETZKY**

Rating: 1 2 3 4 5 Date Used:

468.

**IT IS BETTER TO ASK
TWICE THAN TO LOSE
YOUR WAY ONCE
—DANISH PROVERB**

Rating: 1 2 3 4 5 Date Used:

469.

**NEVER INSULT AN
ALLIGATOR UNTIL YOU
YOU ARE ACROSS THE
RIVER—CORDELL HULL**

Rating: 1 2 3 4 5 Date Used:

470.

**THERE ARE MANY
VICTORIES WORSE THAN
ANY DEFEAT
—GEORGE ELIOT**

Rating: 1 2 3 4 5 Date Used:

471.

**WHEN YOUR ONLY TOOL
IS A HAMMER, YOU SEE
EVERY PROBLEM AS A
NAIL—A. MASLOW**

Rating: 1 2 3 4 5 Date Used:

472.

**TV IS A MEDIUM
—IT'S NEITHER RARE
NOR WELL DONE
—ERNIE KOVACS**

Rating: 1 2 3 4 5 Date Used:

473.

**A MAN MUST MAKE
HIS OPPORTUNITY AS
OFT AS FIND IT
—FRANCIS BACON**

Rating: 1 2 3 4 5 Date Used:

474.

**TO ONE WHO IS
AFRAID EVERYTHING
RUSTLES
—SOPHOCLES**

Rating: 1   2   3   4   5   Date Used:

475.

**WE ARE SOMETIMES
STIRRED BY EMOTION
AND TAKE IT FOR ZEAL
—THOMAS A KEMPIS**

Rating: 1   2   3   4   5   Date Used:

476.

**LIFE IS TOO SHORT
TO BE LITTLE
—B. DISRAELI**

Rating: 1   2   3   4   5   Date Used:

477.

**IT IS NOT THE PART
OF FAITH TO QUESTION,
BUT TO OBEY
—A. B. SIMPSON**

Rating: 1   2   3   4   5   Date Used:

478.

**BE THE CHANGE YOU
WANT TO SEE IN THE
WORLD—M. GANDHI**

Rating: 1   2   3   4   5   Date Used:

479.

**MATERIALISM IS
A SLAVEMASTER—
WE CAN NEVER
GET ENOUGH**

Rating: 1   2   3   4   5   Date Used:

480.

**THIS WORLD IS NOT
MY HOME—I'M JUST
PASSING THROUGH
—THANK GOD!**

Rating: 1   2   3   4   5   Date Used:

481.

**SEE EVERY DAY
AS FROM GOD—
BECAUSE IT IS**

Rating: 1   2   3   4   5   Date Used:

482.

**DOUBTS AND FEARS
CRUMBLE UNDER
THE WEIGHT OF
GOD'S PROMISES**

Rating: 1   2   3   4   5   Date Used:

483.

**BELIEVERS MUST DO TWO
THINGS CONSISTENTLY—
PRAISE GOD
AND CONDEMN EVIL**

Rating: 1   2   3   4   5   Date Used:

484.

**WHERE ALL
THINK ALIKE
NO ONE
THINKS MUCH**

Rating: 1   2   3   4   5   Date Used:

485.

**REVERENCE FOR GOD
GIVES STRENGTH
TO FACE FEARS**

Rating: 1   2   3   4   5   Date Used:

486.   **LOVE HAS A
BAD HABIT
OF GIVING
POP QUIZZES**

Rating: 1   2   3   4   5   Date Used:

487.   **ONE THING YOU
CAN GIVE AND STILL
KEEP IS YOUR WORD**

Rating: 1   2   3   4   5   Date Used:

488.   **A PERSON WHO
THROWS MUD
LOSES GROUND**

Rating: 1   2   3   4   5   Date Used:

489.   **LIFE'S GREATEST
TRAGEDY WOULD BE
TO LOSE GOD
AND NOT MISS HIM**

Rating: 1   2   3   4   5   Date Used:

490.   **THE OPPOSITE OF
BRAVERY IS NOT
COWARDICE BUT
CONFORMITY**

Rating: 1   2   3   4   5   Date Used:

491.   **ONE WHO RETURNS
GOOD FOR EVIL
WINS THE VICTORY**

Rating: 1   2   3   4   5   Date Used:

492.

**TO LIVE FOR SELF
OR LIVE FOR GOD
IS THE CHOICE
WE ALL MAKE**

Rating: 1 2 3 4 5 Date Used:

493.

**TO WALK ON WATER
YOU MUST FIRST
GET OUT OF THE BOAT**

Rating: 1 2 3 4 5 Date Used:

494.

**TRUE JUSTICE BRINGS
JOY TO THE RIGHTEOUS
AND FEAR TO THE EVIL**

Rating: 1 2 3 4 5 Date Used:

495.

**TO SEEK GOOD
YOU MUST FIRST
SEEK GOD**

Rating: 1 2 3 4 5 Date Used:

496.

**DON'T CONFUSE FAME
WITH SUCCESS, MADONNA
IS ONE, MOTHER TERESA
IS THE OTHER**

Rating: 1 2 3 4 5 Date Used:

497.

**LIVE EACH DAY AS IF
IT WERE THE FIRST
OF YOUR MARRIAGE AND
LAST OF YOUR VACATION**

Rating: 1 2 3 4 5 Date Used:

498. **DON'T GIVE AN ALIBI
—GIVE ANOTHER TRY**

Rating: 1   2   3   4   5   Date Used:

499. **CHRISTIANS ARE
THE YEAST IN
THE BREAD OF LIFE
NOT THE CRUST**

Rating: 1   2   3   4   5   Date Used:

500. **IF IGNORANCE IS
BLISS WHY AREN'T
MORE PEOPLE HAPPY?**

Rating: 1   2   3   4   5   Date Used:

501. **DON'T GO TO YOUR
GRAVE WITH YOUR
MUSIC STILL INSIDE**

Rating: 1   2   3   4   5   Date Used:

502. **DON'T CRY BECAUSE
IT'S OVER—SMILE
BECAUSE IT HAPPENED**

Rating: 1   2   3   4   5   Date Used:

503. **CRAYONS ARE DIVERSE
BUT THEY LIVE
IN THE SAME BOX**

Rating: 1   2   3   4   5   Date Used:

504. **MAKE EVERYTHING
AS SIMPLE AS POSSIBLE
—BUT NO SIMPLER**

Rating: 1   2   3   4   5   Date Used:

505. **A TRULY HAPPY PERSON
ENJOYS THE SCENERY
ON A DETOUR**

Rating: 1   2   3   4   5   Date Used:

506. **HAPPINESS OFTEN
COMES THROUGH DOORS
YOU DIDN'T KNOW YOU
HAD LEFT OPEN**

Rating: 1   2   3   4   5   Date Used:

507. **FAITH MAKES THE
UPLOOK GOOD, THE
OUTLOOK GREAT, AND
THE FUTURE GLORIOUS**

Rating: 1   2   3   4   5   Date Used:

508. **THERE IS NO GREAT
FUTURE FOR ANY
PEOPLE WHOSE FAITH
HAS BURNED OUT**

Rating: 1   2   3   4   5   Date Used:

509. **CHRISTIANS SHOULD
HAVE AN ATTITUDE
OF GRATITUDE AND
SERVITUDE**

Rating: 1   2   3   4   5   Date Used:

510. **LIVE WELL—YOUR CAR
ISN'T THE ONLY THING
THAT CAN BE RECALLED**

Rating: 1   2   3   4   5   Date Used:

511.

YOU CAN'T RECYCLE
WASTED TIME

Rating: 1 2 3 4 5 Date Used:

512.

NEVER GIVE THE DEVIL
A RIDE—HE ALWAYS
WANTS TO DRIVE

Rating: 1 2 3 4 5 Date Used:

513.

THEY WHO
ANGER YOU
CONTROL YOU

Rating: 1 2 3 4 5 Date Used:

514.

WORRY IS THE
DARKROOM
WHERE NEGATIVES
ARE DEVELOPED

Rating: 1 2 3 4 5 Date Used:

515.

EVERY STEP TOWARD CHRIST
KILLS A DOUBT

Rating: 1 2 3 4 5 Date Used:

516.

NOT CHOOSING
IS AN IMPORTANT
CHOICE

Rating: 1 2 3 4 5 Date Used:

517.

THERE ARE NO CROWN
WEARERS IN HEAVEN
WHO WERE NOT
CROSS BEARERS HERE

Rating: 1 2 3 4 5 Date Used:

518.

**MENTIONING THE
FAULTS OF OTHERS
DOES NOT RID US
OF OUR OWN**

Rating: 1   2   3   4   5   Date Used:

519.

**CHRISTIANITY HAS
NOT BEEN TRIED AND
FOUND WANTING—IT
HAS NOT BEEN TRIED**

Rating: 1   2   3   4   5   Date Used:

520.

**THIS WEEK'S MESSAGE
WILL BE GIVEN
INSIDE ON SUNDAY**

Rating: 1   2   3   4   5   Date Used:

521.

**WHERE CHRIST IS
HEARD IN THE
PUBLIC HALLS
GOD WILL BLESS**

Rating: 1   2   3   4   5   Date Used:

522.

**CORRUPT LEADERS
ARE ELECTED
NOT BY BRIBES
BUT BY APATHY**

Rating: 1   2   3   4   5   Date Used:

523.

**IF WE FORGET WE ARE
ONE NATION UNDER
GOD WE WILL BE A
NATION GONE UNDER**

Rating: 1   2   3   4   5   Date Used:

524.   **LIFE IS FRAGILE—
                                    HANDLE WITH PRAYER**

Rating: 1   2   3   4   5   Date Used:

525.   **LAZINESS AND POVERTY
                                    ARE COUSINS**

Rating: 1   2   3   4   5   Date Used:

526.   **EACH TIME
                                    YOU SPEAK,
                                    YOUR MIND IS
                                    ON PARADE**

Rating: 1   2   3   4   5   Date Used:

527.   **THEY WHO BURY
                                    THEIR TALENTS
                                    MAKE A GRAVE
                                    MISTAKE**

Rating: 1   2   3   4   5   Date Used:

528.   **YOU CAN GAIN MORE
                                    IN ONE HOUR WITH
                                    GOD THAN IN A
                                    LIFETIME ALONE**

Rating: 1   2   3   4   5   Date Used:

529.   **LEARN TO VALUE
                                    THE DIFFERENCES
                                    IN OTHERS**

Rating: 1   2   3   4   5   Date Used:

530.
RUNNING UP STAIRS
AND RUNNING DOWN
PEOPLE PUTS STRAIN
ON THE HEART

Rating: 1   2   3   4   5   Date Used:

531.
THE BEST WAY
TO GET EVEN
IS TO FORGET

Rating: 1   2   3   4   5   Date Used:

532.
NO CHILD OF GOD
SINS ENOUGH
TO GO BEYOND
FORGIVENESS

Rating: 1   2   3   4   5   Date Used:

533.
ONE WHO IS
WRAPPED UP IN
SELF MAKES A VERY
SMALL PACKAGE

Rating: 1   2   3   4   5   Date Used:

534.
FRIENDSHIP
IS ONE MIND
IN TWO BODIES

Rating: 1   2   3   4   5   Date Used:

535.
FRIENDS ARE GOD'S
WAY OF TAKING
CARE OF US

Rating: 1   2   3   4   5   Date Used:

536.

**FRIENDSHIP IS LIKE
HEALTH, IT IS OFTEN
ONLY VALUED WHEN
IT IS LOST**

Rating: 1   2   3   4   5   Date Used:

537.

**THE LORD GAVE NOAH
THE RAINBOW SIGN
—NOT WATER BUT
FIRE NEXT TIME**

Rating: 1   2   3   4   5   Date Used:

538.

**COME IN AND LET
US PREPARE YOU
FOR YOUR FINALS**

Rating: 1   2   3   4   5   Date Used:

539.

**IF YOU ARE
PLOTTING REVENGE
DIG A GRAVE
FOR TWO**

Rating: 1   2   3   4   5   Date Used:

540.

**GOD SUPPLIES
OUR NEEDS—
NOT OUR GREEDS**

Rating: 1   2   3   4   5   Date Used:

541.

**ALL WORRY IS
ATHEISM—A WANT
OF TRUST IN GOD**

Rating: 1   2   3   4   5   Date Used:

542.

**HE IS MOST EMPTY
WHO IS FULL
OF HIMSELF**

Rating: 1   2   3   4   5   Date Used:

543.

**EVERY BIT OF LOVE
ON EARTH HAS GOD
AT THE OTHER
END OF IT**

Rating: 1   2   3   4   5   Date Used:

544.

**ONE OF LIFE'S GREAT
PRIVILEGES IS
TO HAVE INSTANT
ACCESS TO GOD**

Rating: 1   2   3   4   5   Date Used:

545.

**SERVICE IS NOT A LIST
OF THINGS TO DO—
IT IS A WAY OF LIFE**

Rating: 1   2   3   4   5   Date Used:

546.

**DON'T SHOOT AT
RESCUERS IF YOU ARE
ON A SINKING SHIP**

Rating: 1   2   3   4   5   Date Used:

547.

**HOPE TIES US
TO THE FUTURE
AS MEMORY TIES US
TO THE PAST**

Rating: 1   2   3   4   5   Date Used:

548.

**LET NAIL-PIERCED HANDS
HAVE THE WHEEL AND
YOU WILL BE SAFE**

Rating: 1   2   3   4   5   Date Used:

549.

**TRIALS TEST OUR FAITH
AND STRENGTHEN
OUR SPIRIT**

Rating: 1   2   3   4   5   Date Used:

550.

**THE WAGES OF SIN
IS DEATH—THERE IS
NO MINIMUM WAGE**

Rating: 1   2   3   4   5   Date Used:

551.

**ANGER ALWAYS HAS
REASONS BUT
SELDOM GOOD ONES**

Rating: 1   2   3   4   5   Date Used:

552.

**UTTERMOST LOVE
TOOK THE
UTTERMOST RISK
ON THE CROSS**

Rating: 1   2   3   4   5   Date Used:

553.

**NO ONE KNOWS
HOW BAD THEY ARE
UNTIL THEY TRY
TO BE GOOD**

Rating: 1   2   3   4   5   Date Used:

554.

CHRISTIANS NEVER MEET FOR THE LAST TIME

Rating: 1   2   3   4   5   Date Used:

555.

CHRIST BRINGS INNER PEACE THAT PASSES UNDERSTANDING

Rating: 1   2   3   4 . 5   Date Used:

556.

CHRISTIANS AREN'T PERFECT—THEY ARE JUST FORGIVEN

Rating: 1   2   3   4   5   Date Used:

557.

SIN NEVER COMES DRESSED IN BLACK IT'S MOST OFTEN DRESSED IN WHITE

Rating: 1   2   3   4   5   Date Used:

558.

SIN IS MOST EFFECTIVE WHEN IT COMES DRESSED IN HALF TRUTH

Rating: 1   2   3   4   5   Date Used:

559.

APART FROM GOD EVERY ACTIVITY IS A PASSING WHIFF OF INSIGNIFICANCE

Rating: 1   2   3   4   5   Date Used:

560.   **FOR FAST RELIEF TAKE
TWO TABLETS—THE
10 COMMANDMENTS**

Rating: 1   2   3   4   5   Date Used:

561.   **GET IN TOUCH WITH
GOD THROUGH
KNEE-MAIL**

Rating: 1   2   3   4   5   Date Used:

562.   **ROCK BOTTOM
IS NOT SO BAD
IF YOU ARE STANDING
ON CHRIST THE ROCK**

Rating: 1   2   3   4   5   Date Used:

563.   **GOD BRINGS OUT
ONLY THE BEST
IN YOU**

Rating: 1   2   3   4   5   Date Used:

564.   **GOD DWELLS
WHEREVER PEOPLE
LET HIM IN**

Rating: 1   2   3   4   5   Date Used:

565.   **THERE IS A
WORLDLY TRINITY—
ME, MYSELF,
AND I**

Rating: 1   2   3   4   5   Date Used:

566.
TIME FLIES BY
EVEN WHEN YOU'RE
NOT HAVING FUN

Rating: 1   2   3   4   5   Date Used:

567.
ADULTERY—
JUST SAY NO

Rating: 1   2   3   4   5   Date Used:

568.
MATURE WISDOM CAN
OFTEN BE CONFUSED
WITH BEING TOO TIRED

Rating: 1   2   3   4   5   Date Used:

569.
GOD NEVER CALLS US
TO DO THINGS IN
OUR OWN STRENGTH

Rating: 1   2   3   4   5   Date Used:

570.
MOSES, DAVID, AND
GIDEON LEARNED
THAT GOD IS
ALWAYS ENOUGH

Rating: 1   2   3   4   5   Date Used:

571.
GOD'S LOVE IS
UNCONDITIONAL; HOW
COULD WE ASK FOR
MORE?—KAY ARTHUR

Rating: 1   2   3   4   5   Date Used:

572.

IN THE MUSTARD SEED
GOD SEES THE TREE
—C. H. SPURGEON

Rating: 1 2 3 4 5 Date Used:

573.

HE WHO ACCUSES ALL
OF MANKIND ACCUSES
ONLY ONE
—EDMUND BURKE

Rating: 1 2 3 4 5 Date Used:

574.

THE PRINCIPAL PART
OF FAITH IS PATIENCE
—GEORGE MACDONALD

Rating: 1 2 3 4 5 Date Used:

575.

BE NOT AFRAID TO GO
SLOWLY—BE ONLY
AFRAID OF STANDING
STILL—JAPANESE PROVERB

Rating: 1 2 3 4 5 Date Used:

576.

ONLY A VIRTUOUS
PEOPLE ARE CAPABLE
OF FREEDOM
—BENJAMIN FRANKLIN

Rating: 1 2 3 4 5 Date Used:

577.

FOR EVERY MAN
IT MUST BE
CHRIST OR TRAGEDY
—A. W. TOZER

Rating: 1 2 3 4 5 Date Used:

578.   **THE POOR SEE BETTER
—THROUGH THEIR PAIN
THEY SEE GOD CLEARLY
—MOTHER TERESA**

Rating: 1   2   3   4   5   Date Used:

579.   **FIND THE GOOD AND
PRAISE IT—ALEX HALEY**

Rating: 1   2   3   4   5   Date Used:

580.   **OH, GOD, I HAVE NO
REST UNTIL I FIND REST
IN YOU—AUGUSTINE**

Rating: 1   2   3   4   5   Date Used:

581.   **WHO BEST BEAR HIS
MILD YOKE, THEY
SERVE HIM BEST
—JOHN MILTON**

Rating: 1   2   3   4   5   Date Used:

582.   **NO LEGACY IS SO
RICH AS HONESTY
—SHAKESPEARE**

Rating: 1   2   3   4   5   Date Used:

583.   **TACT: THE ABILITY TO
DESCRIBE OTHERS AS
THEY SEE THEMSELVES
—A. LINCOLN**

Rating: 1   2   3   4   5   Date Used:

584.

**WELL DONE IS
BETTER THAN WELL
SAID—B. FRANKLIN**

Rating: 1   2   3   4   5   Date Used:

585.

**THE PRICE OF
GREATNESS IS
RESPONSIBILITY
—W. CHURCHILL**

Rating: 1   2   3   4   5   Date Used:

586.

**IF THERE'S A WAY
TO DO BETTER
FIND IT—T. EDISON**

Rating: 1   2   3   4   5   Date Used:

587.

**A MAN'S BEST GIFT
TO HIS CHILDREN
IS TO LOVE
THEIR MOTHER**

Rating: 1   2   3   4   5   Date Used:

588.

**WORDS ARE WINDOWS
TO THE HEART**

Rating: 1   2   3   4   5   Date Used:

589.

**THE CHIEF DUTY
OF LOVE
IS TO LISTEN**

Rating: 1   2   3   4   5   Date Used:

590.

**PEOPLE WHO SAY
GOD IS DEAD AND
ELVIS IS ALIVE
CAN'T BE TOO BRIGHT**

Rating: 1   2   3   4   5   Date Used:

591.

**YOU ARE RICHER TODAY
IF YOU HAVE LAUGHED,
SUNG, GIVEN, OR
FORGIVEN**

Rating: 1   2   3   4   5   Date Used:

592.

**AT THE END
OF YOUR ROPE
THERE IS GOD
AND HOPE**

Rating: 1   2   3   4   5   Date Used:

593.

**SAINTS DON'T THINK
LESS OF THEMSELVES
—THEY THINK OF
THEMSELVES LESS**

Rating: 1   2   3   4   5   Date Used:

594.

**1 CROSS
3 NAILS
4 GIVENESS**

Rating: 1   2   3   4   5   Date Used:

595.

**DON'T WAIT FOR
SIX STRONG MEN
TO TAKE YOU
TO CHURCH**

Rating: 1   2   3   4   5   Date Used:

596.

**PRAYER ENLARGES
THE HEART UNTIL
IT CAN CONTAIN
GOD'S GIFT OF HIMSELF**

Rating: 1   2   3   4   5   Date Used:

597.

**WHAT HE WILLS—
NOTHING MORE
NOTHING LESS
NOTHING ELSE**

Rating: 1   2   3   4   5   Date Used:

598.

**WALK IN GOD'S WAYS
AND YOU WILL TRULY
APPRECIATE ALL THE
DAYS HE GIVES YOU**

Rating: 1   2   3   4   5   Date Used:

599.

**GOD REIGNS
IN THE HEARTS
OF HIS SERVANTS**

Rating: 1   2   3   4   5   Date Used:

600.

**FAILURE IS ALWAYS
AN EVENT—
NOT A PERSON**

Rating: 1   2   3   4   5   Date Used:

601.

**WISE PEOPLE
SEEK ADVICE FROM
WISER PEOPLE**

Rating: 1   2   3   4   5   Date Used:

602.

**BY TRIALS
GOD SHAPES US
FOR HIGHER THINGS**

Rating: 1   2   3   4   5   Date Used:

603.

**JESUS IS RIGHT FOR
WHATEVER IS WRONG**

Rating: 1   2   3   4   5   Date Used:

604.

**IT IS FAR BETTER
TO DIE WELL
THAN TO LIVE ILL**

Rating: 1   2   3   4   5   Date Used:

605.

**A NATION THAT TURNS
TO GOD ONLY IN
TROUBLE INVITES
MORE TROUBLE**

Rating: 1   2   3   4   5   Date Used:

606.

**GOD INVENTED
FREEDOM SO LOVE
MIGHT BE PERFECT**

Rating: 1   2   3   4   5   Date Used:

607.

**GOD HAS PLANTED
A GARDEN FOR US
BUT WE HAVE THE JOB
OF WEEDING**

Rating: 1   2   3   4   5   Date Used:

608.

THERE IS LIFE
IN A LOOK
AT JESUS

Rating: 1   2   3   4   5   Date Used:

609.

IF YOU DON'T KNOW
THE MOUNTAIN PATH
YOU'D BETTER KNOW
THE RIGHT GUIDE

Rating: 1   2   3   4   5   Date Used:

610.

GOD NEVER ASKS
THAT WE KISS
OUR BRAINS GOOD-BYE

Rating: 1   2   3   4   5   Date Used:

611.

IT'S A TREAT
NOT A TRICK —
GOD LOVES YOU

Rating: 1   2   3   4   5   Date Used:

612.

A REAL THANKSGIVING
IS CELEBRATED IN
REAL THANKSGIVING

Rating: 1   2   3   4   5   Date Used:

613.

DO YOU HAVE ROOM
FOR JESUS?

Rating: 1   2   3   4   5   Date Used:

614.

I'M ALSO MAKING A
LIST AND CHECKING
IT TWICE—GOD

Rating: 1   2   3   4   5   Date Used:

615. **LIFE DOES NOT HAVE
TO BE PERFECT TO
BE WONDERFUL**

Rating: 1   2   3   4   5   Date Used:

616. **XMAS IS THE SEASON
WITHOUT THE REASON**

Rating: 1   2   3   4   5   Date Used:

617. **THE SOURCE OF
TRUTH COMES
IN A BOOK
AND A BABY**

Rating: 1   2   3   4   5   Date Used:

618. **UNTO US A SON IS GIVEN
HE HAS COME FROM
GOD'S OWN HEAVEN**

Rating: 1   2   3   4   5   Date Used:

619. **ADVENT—THE PAUSE
THAT REFRESHES**

Rating: 1   2   3   4   5   Date Used:

620. **MERRY CHRISTMAS
FELIZ NAVIDAD
JOYEUX NOEL
FROELICHE WEIHNACTEN**

Rating: 1   2   3   4   5   Date Used:

621. **THE IDEAL GIFT—
A HUG—
ONE SIZE FITS ALL**

Rating: 1   2   3   4   5   Date Used:

622.

**LENT IS
SPRING TRAINING
FOR THE CHRISTIAN**

Rating: 1   2   3   4   5   Date Used:

623.

**LOVE'S NAILS HELD HIM
ON THE CROSS**

Rating: 1   2   3   4   5   Date Used:

624.

**EASTER AND SPRING
ARE JUST TWO OF GOD'S
WAYS OF SAYING
HE LOVES US**

Rating: 1   2   3   4   5   Date Used:

625.

**EASTER IS MORE THAN
SOMETHING TO DYE FOR**

Rating: 1   2   3   4   5   Date Used:

626.

**EVERY FLOWER OF
SPRINGTIME SPEAKS
OF THE RESURRECTION**

Rating: 1   2   3   4   5   Date Used:

627.

**ETERNAL HOPE IS
THE MESSAGE OF THE
RESURRECTION!**

Rating: 1   2   3   4   5   Date Used:

628.

**A MOTHER HOLDS HER
CHILDREN'S HANDS FOR
A WHILE BUT THEIR
HEARTS FOREVER**

Rating: 1   2   3   4   5   Date Used:

629.

**TASTE AND SEE THAT
THE LORD IS GOOD
—PS. 34:8**

Rating: 1   2   3   4   5   Date Used:

630.

**SEEK PEACE
AND PURSUE IT
—PS. 34:14**

Rating: 1   2   3   4   5   Date Used:

631.

**DELIGHT YOURSELF IN
THE LORD AND HE WILL
GIVE YOU THE DESIRES
OF YOUR HEART—PS. 37:4**

Rating: 1   2   3   4   5   Date Used:

632.

**BE STILL BEFORE THE
LORD AND WAIT
PATIENTLY FOR HIM
—PS. 37:7**

Rating: 1   2   3   4   5   Date Used:

633.

**IN YOUR NAME
I WILL HOPE
FOR YOUR NAME
IS GOOD—PS. 52:9**

Rating: 1   2   3   4   5   Date Used:

634.

**BLESSED IS THE MAN
WHO FEARS THE LORD
—PS. 112:1**

Rating: 1   2   3   4   5   Date Used:

635.

YOUR WORD HAVE I HID
IN MY HEART THAT
I MIGHT NOT SIN
AGAINST THEE—PS. 119:11

Rating: 1   2   3   4   5   Date Used:

636.

BLESSED ARE YOU
O LORD—TEACH ME
YOUR STATUTES
—PS. 119:12

Rating: 1   2   3   4   5   Date Used:

637.

YOU ARE MY REFUGE
AND MY SHIELD—I PUT
MY HOPE IN YOUR WORD
—PS. 119:114

Rating: 1   2   3   4   5   Date Used:

638.

CHILDREN ARE
A HERITAGE
FROM THE LORD
—PS. 127:3

Rating: 1   2   3   4   5   Date Used:

639.

THOUGH THE LORD IS
ON HIGH HE LOOKS
UPON THE LOWLY
—PS. 138:6

Rating: 1   2   3   4   5   Date Used:

640.

HOW PRECIOUS TO ME
ARE YOUR THOUGHTS,
O GOD —PS. 139:17

Rating: 1   2   3   4   5   Date Used:

641.

**IN ALL YOUR WAYS
ACKNOWLEDGE GOD AND
HE WILL MAKE YOUR PATHS
STRAIGHT—PROV. 3:6**

Rating: 1   2   3   4   5   Date Used:

642.

**HOLD ON TO
INSTRUCTION . . .
FOR IT IS YOUR LIFE
—PROV. 4:13**

Rating: 1   2   3   4   5   Date Used:

643.

**A MAN WHO COMMITS
ADULTERY LACKS JUDGMENT
. . . HE DESTROYS HIMSELF
—PROV. 6:32**

Rating: 1   2   3   4   5   Date Used:

644.

**HE WHO
GUARDS HIS LIPS
GUARDS HIS LIFE
—PROV. 13:3**

Rating: 1   2   3   4   5   Date Used:

645.

**A QUICK-TEMPERED
MAN DOES
FOOLISH THINGS
—PROV. 14:17**

Rating: 1   2   3   4   5   Date Used:

646.

**THE JUST MAN WALKS
IN HIS INTEGRITY
HIS CHILDREN ARE
BLESSED—PROV. 20:7**

Rating: 1   2   3   4   5   Date Used:

647. **AS IRON SHARPENS
IRON SO ONE MAN
SHARPENS ANOTHER
—PROV. 27:17**

Rating: 1   2   3   4   5   Date Used:

648. **HE WHO HARDENS
HIS HEART FALLS
INTO TROUBLE
—PROV. 28:14**

Rating: 1   2   3   4   5   Date Used:

649. **WISE MEN TURN
AWAY ANGER
—PROV. 29:8**

Rating: 1   2   3   4   5   Date Used:

650. **A GOOD NAME
IS BETTER THAN
FINE PERFUME
—ECCL. 7:1**

Rating: 1   2   3   4   5   Date Used:

651. **THOUGH YOUR SINS ARE
LIKE SCARLET, THEY
SHALL BE AS WHITE AS
SNOW—ISA. 1:18**

Rating: 1   2   3   4   5   Date Used:

652. **SEEK THE LORD
WHILE HE MAY BE FOUND
CALL ON HIM WHILE
HE IS NEAR —ISA. 55:6**

Rating: 1   2   3   4   5   Date Used:

653.   **EVERYONE WHOSE
NAME IS FOUND WRITTEN
IN THE BOOK WILL BE
DELIVERED—DAN. 12:1**

Rating: 1   2   3   4   5   Date Used:

654.   **NOT BY MIGHT NOR BY
POWER BUT BY MY
SPIRIT, SAYS THE LORD
—ZECH. 4:6**

Rating: 1   2   3   4   5   Date Used:

655.   **MY YOKE IS EASY
AND MY BURDEN IS
LIGHT—MATT. 11:30**

Rating: 1   2   3   4   5   Date Used:

656.   **IF YOU HAVE FAITH
AS SMALL AS A MUSTARD
SEED. . . NOTHING WILL BE
IMPOSSIBLE—MATT. 17:20**

Rating: 1   2   3   4   5   Date Used:

657.   **BLESSED IS HE
WHO COMES IN THE
NAME OF THE LORD
—MATT. 21:9**

Rating: 1   2   3   4   5   Date Used:

658.   **THE GREATEST AMONG
YOU WILL BE YOUR
SERVANT—MATT. 23:11**

Rating: 1   2   3   4   5   Date Used:

659.
**FOR NOTHING IS
IMPOSSIBLE WITH GOD
—LUKE 1:37**

Rating: 1   2   3   4   5   Date Used:

660.
**LOVE YOUR ENEMIES
DO GOOD TO THOSE
WHO HATE YOU
—LUKE 6:27**

Rating: 1   2   3   4   5   Date Used:

661.
**HE WHO IS FAITHFUL
IN A SMALL THING IS
FAITHFUL ALSO IN
MUCH—LUKE 16:10**

Rating: 1   2   3   4   5   Date Used:

662.
**BY STANDING FIRM
YOU WILL GAIN LIFE
—LUKE 21:19**

Rating: 1   2   3   4   5   Date Used:

663.
**WHOEVER REJECTS
THE SON
WILL NOT SEE LIFE
—JOHN 3:36**

Rating: 1   2   3   4   5   Date Used:

664.
**MY FATHER WILL
HONOR THE ONE
WHO SERVES ME
—JESUS IN JOHN 12:26**

Rating: 1   2   3   4   5   Date Used:

665.

**SANCTIFY THEM
BY THE TRUTH—
YOUR WORD IS TRUTH
—JESUS IN JOHN 17:17**

Rating: 1   2   3   4   5   Date Used:

666.

**HE PROVIDES PLENTY
OF FOOD AND FILLS
YOUR HEARTS WITH JOY
—ACTS 14:17**

Rating: 1   2   3   4   5   Date Used:

667.

**I AM NOT ASHAMED
OF THE GOSPEL. . . . IT IS
THE POWER OF GOD
—ROM. 1:16**

Rating: 1   2   3   4   5   Date Used:

668.

**SIN SHALL NOT BE
YOUR MASTER BECAUSE
YOU ARE . . . UNDER
GRACE—ROM. 6:14**

Rating: 1   2   3   4   5   Date Used:

669.

**THE MIND CONTROLLED
BY THE SPIRIT IS
LIFE AND PEACE —ROM. 8:6**

Rating: 1   2   3   4   5   Date Used:

670.

**EVERYONE WHO CALLS
ON THE NAME
OF THE LORD WILL BE
SAVED—ROM. 10:13**

Rating: 1   2   3   4   5   Date Used:

671.

**DO NOT CONFORM
ANY LONGER TO THE
PATTERN OF THIS
WORLD—ROM. 12:2**

Rating: 1   2   3   4   5   Date Used:

672.

**IN CHRIST WE . . . FORM
ONE BODY, AND EACH
MEMBER BELONGS TO ALL
THE OTHERS—ROM. 12:5**

Rating: 1   2   3   4   5   Date Used:

673.

**HAS NOT GOD MADE
FOOLISH THE WISDOM
OF THE WORLD?
—1 COR. 1:20**

Rating: 1   2   3   4   5   Date Used:

674.

**THE FOOLISHNESS OF
GOD IS WISER THAN
MAN'S WISDOM
—1 COR. 1:25**

Rating: 1   2   3   4   5   Date Used:

675.

**CHRIST JESUS . . .
OUR RIGHTEOUSNESS,
HOLINESS, AND
REDEMPTION—1 COR. 1:30**

Rating: 1   2   3   4   5   Date Used:

676.

**LOVE IS PATIENT . . .
IT KEEPS NO RECORD
OF WRONGS
—1 COR. 13:4–5**

Rating: 1   2   3   4   5   Date Used:

677.

**GOD LOVES
A CHEERFUL GIVER
—2 COR. 9:7**

Rating: 1   2   3   4   5   Date Used:

678.

**SERVE
ONE ANOTHER
IN LOVE
—GAL. 5:13**

Rating: 1   2   3   4   5   Date Used:

679.

**BY GRACE
YOU HAVE BEEN SAVED
. . . NOT BY WORKS
—EPH. 2:8–9**

Rating: 1   2   3   4   5   Date Used:

680.

**SPEAKING THE TRUTH
IN LOVE, WE WILL . . .
GROW UP INTO HIM
—EPH. 4:15**

Rating: 1   2   3   4   5   Date Used:

681.

**DO NOT LET THE SUN
GO DOWN ON YOUR
ANGER—EPH. 4:26**

Rating: 1   2   3   4   5   Date Used:

682.

**HE WHO BEGAN
A GOOD WORK IN YOU
WILL PERFECT IT
—PHIL. 1:6**

Rating: 1   2   3   4   5   Date Used:

683.
IT IS GOD WHO WORKS IN YOU . . . ACCORDING TO HIS GOOD PURPOSE
—PHIL. 2:13

Rating: 1 2 3 4 5 Date Used:

684.
GOD WILL MEET ALL YOUR NEEDS . . . IN CHRIST JESUS
—PHIL. 4:19

Rating: 1 2 3 4 5 Date Used:

685.
CHRIST IN YOU THE HOPE OF GLORY
—COL. 1:27

Rating: 1 2 3 4 5 Date Used:

686.
SET YOUR MINDS ON THINGS ABOVE NOT ON EARTHLY THINGS
—COL. 3:2

Rating: 1 2 3 4 5 Date Used:

687.
ABOVE ALL ELSE PUT ON LOVE
—COL. 3:14

Rating: 1 2 3 4 5 Date Used:

688.
LET THE PEACE OF CHRIST RULE IN YOUR HEARTS
—COL. 3:15

Rating: 1 2 3 4 5 Date Used:

689.

LET THE WORD
OF CHRIST
DWELL IN YOU RICHLY
—COL. 3:16

Rating: 1   2   3   4   5   Date Used:

690.

TEST EVERYTHING
HOLD ON TO THE GOOD
—1 THESS. 5:21

Rating: 1   2   3   4   5   Date Used:

691.

MAY THE LORD DIRECT
YOUR HEARTS INTO
GOD'S LOVE
—2 THESS. 3:5

Rating: 1   2   3   4   5   Date Used:

692.

GOD WANTS ALL . . .
TO COME TO A
KNOWLEDGE OF THE TRUTH
—1 TIM. 2:3–4

Rating: 1   2   3   4   5   Date Used:

693.

BE STRONG
IN THE GRACE
THAT IS IN CHRIST
—2 TIM. 2:1

Rating: 1   2   3   4   5   Date Used:

694.

WITHOUT FAITH
IT IS IMPOSSIBLE
TO PLEASE GOD
—HEB. 11:6

Rating: 1   2   3   4   5   Date Used:

695.   **BE CONTENT WITH
WHAT YOU HAVE
—HEB. 13:5**

Rating: 1   2   3   4   5   Date Used:

696.   **THROUGH JESUS . . .
LET US CONTINUALLY
OFFER GOD A SACRIFICE
OF PRAISE—HEB. 13:15**

Rating: 1   2   3   4   5   Date Used:

697.   **IF ANY LACK WISDOM
ASK GOD . . . AND
IT WILL BE GIVEN
—JAMES 1:5**

Rating: 1   2   3   4   5   Date Used:

698.   **GOD OPPOSES THE
PROUD BUT GIVES
GRACE TO THE HUMBLE
—JAMES 4:6**

Rating: 1   2   3   4   5   Date Used:

699.   **YOUR FAITH AND
HOPE ARE IN GOD
—1 PETER 1:21**

Rating: 1   2   3   4   5   Date Used:

700.   **SINCE GOD SO LOVED
US WE ALSO OUGHT TO
LOVE ONE ANOTHER
—1 JOHN 4:11**

Rating: 1   2   3   4   5   Date Used:

701.

LET WHOEVER WISHES TAKE THE FREE GIFT OF THE WATER OF LIFE—REV. 22:17

Rating: 1   2   3   4   5   Date Used:

A third volume of *Sentence Sermons* is being developed by Dr. Harvey. You are invited to participate. This volume will again include stories that tell of the impact of sentence sermons on people's lives. If you have a sentence sermon or a story you would like to submit for possible publication, please mail it to:

Dr. L. James Harvey
6732 Gracepoint Drive
Caledonia, MI 49316

or by e-mail to: jharvey@kregel.com

All submissions are subject to editing and cannot be returned. You will be notified if your item is accepted, and your name will be acknowledged in the book. All rights to submitted material will be retained by the author. Those who have stories published will receive a complimentary copy of the book in lieu of payment.

INDEX

Sentence Sermon Topics and Sources

(listed by sermon number)

139